Lecture Notes in Computer Sci

T0238025

Commenced Publication in 1973
Founding and Former Series Editors:
Gerhard Goos, Juris Hartmanis, and Jan van Leeuwen

Thomas S. Huang   Nicu Sebe
Michael S. Lew   Vladimir Pavlović
Mathias Kölsch   Aphrodite Galata
Branislav Kisačanin (Eds.)

Computer Vision in Human-Computer Interaction

ECCV 2006 Workshop on HCI
Graz, Austria, May 13, 2006
Proceedings

 Springer

Volume Editors

Thomas S. Huang
E-mail: huang@ifp.uiuc.edu

Nicu Sebe
E-mail: nicu@science.uva.nl

Michael S. Lew
E-mail: mlew@liacs.nl

Vladimir Pavlović
E-mail: vladimir@cs.rutgers.edu

Mathias Kölsch
E-mail: kolsch@nps.edu

Aphrodite Galata
E-mail: a.galata@cs.man.ac.uk

Branislav Kisačanin
E-mail: b.kisacanin@ieee.org

Library of Congress Control Number: 2006925105

CR Subject Classification (1998): I.4, I.5, I.3, H.5.2, K.4.2

LNCS Sublibrary: SL 6 – Image Processing, Computer Vision, Pattern Recognition, and Graphics

ISSN   0302-9743
ISBN-10   3-540-34202-8 Springer Berlin Heidelberg New York
ISBN-13   978-3-540-34202-1 Springer Berlin Heidelberg New York

Springer is a part of Springer Science+Business Media

springer.com

© Springer-Verlag Berlin Heidelberg 2006
Printed in Germany

Typesetting: Camera-ready by author, data conversion by Scientific Publishing Services, Chennai, India
Printed on acid-free paper   SPIN: 11754336   06/3142   5 4 3 2 1 0

Preface

The interests and goals of HCI (human–computer interaction) include understanding, designing, building, and evaluating complex interactive systems involving many people and technologies. Developments in software and hardware
technologies are continuously driving applications in supporting our collabora-
tive and communicative needs as social beings, both at work and at play. At
the same time, similar developments are pushing the human–computer interface
beyond the desktop and into our pockets, streets, and buildings. Developments
in mobile, wearable, and pervasive communications and computing technologies
provide exciting challenges and opportunities for HCI.

The present volume represents the proceedings of the HCI 2006 Workshop
that was held in conjunction with ECCV 2006 (European Conference on Computer Vision) in Graz, Austria. The goal of this workshop was to bring together
researchers from the field of computer vision whose work is related to human–
computer interaction. We solicited original contributions that address a wide
range of theoretical and application issues in human–computer interaction.

We were very pleased by the response and had a difficult task of selecting only
11 papers (out of 27 submitted) to be presented at the workshop. The accepted
papers were presented in four sessions, as follows:

Face Analysis

- In their paper "Robust Face Alignment Based On Hierarchical Classifier
  Network" authors Li Zhang, Haizhou Ai, and Shihong Lao build a hierarchical classifier network that connects face detection and face alignment into
  a smooth coarse-to-fine procedure. Thus a robust face alignment algorithm
  on face images with expression and pose changes is introduced. Experiments
  are reported to show its accuracy and robustness.
- In "EigenExpress Approach in Recognition of Facial Expression using GPU"
  authors Qi Wu, Mingli Song, Jiajun Bu, and Chun Chen present an efficient facial expression recognition system based on a GPU-based filter for preprocessing and EigenExpress and Modified Hausdorff distance for classification.
- In "Face Representation Method Using Pixel-to-Vertex Map for 3D Model-
  Based Face Recognition" authors Taehwa Hong, Hagbae Kim, Hyeonjoon
  Moon, Yongguk Kim, Jongweon Lee, and Seungbin Moon describe a 3D face
  representation algorithm to reduce the number of vertices and optimize its
  computation time. They evaluate the performance of the proposed algorithm
  with the Korean face database collected using a stereo-camera-based 3D face
  capturing device.
- In "Robust Head Tracking with Particles Based on Multiple Cues Fusion"
  authors Yuan Li, Haizhou Ai, Chang Huang, and Shihong Lao present a fully
  automatic and highly robust head tracking algorithm that fuses the face cues
  from a real-time multiview face detection with color spatiogram and contour

gradient cues under a particle filter framework. Experiments show that this algorithm is highly robust against target position, size, and pose change, as well as unfavorable conditions such as occlusion, poor illumination, and cluttered background.

Gesture and Emotion Recognition

- In "Vision-Based Interpretation of Hand Gestures for Remote Control of a Computer Mouse" authors Antonis A. Argyros and Manolis I. A. Lourakis present a human–computer interaction system that is capable of recognizing hand gestures and of interpreting them to remotely control a computer mouse. This work is based on their previous work on 2D and 3D tracking of colored objects. Two different gestural vocabularies are investigated, based on 2D and 3D hand information, respectively. Experiments are used to compare these vocabularies in terms of efficiency, robustness, reliability, and ease of use.
- In "Computing Emotion Awareness Through Facial Electromyography" authors Egon van den Broek, Marleen Schut, Joyce Westerink, Jan van Herk, and Kees Tuinenbreijer use coarse time windows to discriminate between positive, negative, neutral, and mixed emotions. They use six parameters (i.e., mean, absolute deviation, standard deviation, variance, skewness, and kurtosis) of three facial EMGs: zygomaticus major, corrugator supercilii, and frontalis. The zygomaticus major is shown to discriminate excellently between the four emotion categories and, consequently, can facilitate empathic HCI.

Event Detection

- In "Silhouette-Based Method for Object Classification and Human Action Recognition in Video" authors Yiğithan Dedeoğlu, B. Uğur Töreyin, Uğur Güdükbay, and A. Enis Çetin present an instance-based machine learning algorithm and a system for real-time object classification and human action recognition which makes use of object silhouettes. An adaptive background subtraction model is used for object segmentation. A supervised learning method based on template matching is adopted to classify objects into classes like human, human group, and vehicle, and human actions into predefined classes like walking, boxing, and kicking.
- In "Voice Activity Detection Using Wavelet-Based Multiresolution Spectrum and Support Vector Machines and Audio Mixing Algorithm" authors Wei Xue, Sidan Du, Chengzhi Fang, and Yingxian Ye present a voice activity detection (VAD) algorithm and efficient speech mixing algorithm for a multimedia conference. The proposed VAD uses MFCC of multiresolution spectrum as features and classifies voice by support vector machines (SVM).
- In "Action Recognition in Broadcast Tennis Video Using Optical Flow and Support Vector Machine" authors Guangyu Zhu, Changsheng Xu, Wen Gao, and Qingming Huang present a novel approach to recognize the basic player actions in broadcast tennis video where the player is only about 30 pixels

tall. A new motion descriptor based on optical flow is proposed where the optical flow is treated as spatial patterns of noisy measurements instead of precise pixel displacements. Support vector machine is employed to train the action classifier.

Applications

- In "FaceMouse — A Human-Computer Interface for Tetraplegic People" authors Emanuele Perini, Simone Soria, Andrea Prati, and Rita Cucchiara propose a new human–machine interface particularly conceived for people with severe disabilities (specifically tetraplegic people), that allows them to interact with the computer. They have studied a new paradigm called "derivative paradigm," where the users indicate the direction along which the mouse pointer must be moved. The system that uses this paradigm consists of a common, low-cost webcam and a set of computer vision techniques developed to identify the parts of the user's face and exploit them for moving the pointer.
- In "Object Retrieval by Query with Sensibility Based on the KANSEI-Vocabulary Scale" authors Sunkyoung Baek, Myunggwon Hwang, Miyoung Cho, Chang Choi, and Pankoo Kim propose the KANSEI-Vocabulary Scale by associating human sensibilities with shapes among visual information. They construct the object retrieval system for evaluation of their approach and are able to retrieve object images with the most appropriate shape in terms of the query's sensibility.

We would like to thank the contributing authors and Springer's LNCS team for their help in preparation of the workshop proceedings. There would not be a workshop to begin with had it not been for the invaluable help we received from the Program Committee members (listed later in the book) and their careful reviews of submitted papers. The review process has been facilitated by the Conference Management Toolkit, a free service provided by Microsoft Research (http://msrcmt.research.microsoft.com/cmt). We would also like to thank the Chairs of the ECCV 2006 Conference in Graz, Austria, for their support and help. Finally, we would like to thank our corporate sponsor, Delphi Corporation, for generous support of the workshop.

May 2006   T.S. Huang
Graz, Austria   N. Sebe
                                                   M.S. Lew
                                                 V. Pavlović
                                                  M. Kölsch
                                                  A. Galata
                                                 B. Kisačanin
                                               HCI 2006 Chairs

Organization

HCI 2006 (Workshop on Human–Computer Interaction) was held in conjunction with ECCV 2006 (European Conference on Computer Vision), on 13 May 2006, in Graz, Austria.

Organizing Committee

General Chair	Thomas S. Huang (University of Illinois at Urbana-Champaign, USA)
Program Chairs	Nicu Sebe (University of Amsterdam, Netherlands)
	Michael S. Lew (University of Leiden, Netherlands)
	Vladimir Pavlović (Rutgers University, USA)
	Mathias Kölsch (Naval Postgraduate School, USA)
Publicity Chairs	Aphrodite Galata (University of Manchester, UK)
	Branislav Kisačanin (Delphi Corporation, USA)

Program Committee

K. Aizawa	A. Hanjalic	Q. Tian
A. del Bimbo	A. Jaimes	M. Turk
N. Boujemaa	A. Kapoor	J. Vitria
I. Cohen	M. Nixon	G. Xu
J. Cohn	M. Pantic	M. Yang
J. Crowley	I. Patras	X. Zhou
D. Gatica-Perez	A. Pentland	
T. Gevers	S. Sclaroff	

Corporate Sponsor

Delphi Corporation, USA
www.delphi.com

Table of Contents

Computer Vision in Human-Computer Interaction

Robust Face Alignment Based on Hierarchical Classifier Network

Li Zhang[1], Haizhou Ai[1], and Shihong Lao[2]

[1] Department of Computer Science, Tsinghua University,
Beijing 100084, China
[2] Sensing and Control Technology Lab, Omron Corporation,
Kyoto 619-0283, Japan
ahz@mail.tsinghua.edu.cn

Abstract. Robust face alignment is crucial for many face processing applications. As face detection only gives a rough estimation of face region, one important problem is how to align facial shapes starting from this rough estimation, especially on face images with expression and pose changes. We propose a novel method of face alignment by building a hierarchical classifier network, connecting face detection and face alignment into a smooth coarse-to-fine procedure. Classifiers are trained to recognize feature textures in different scales from entire face to local patterns. A multi-layer structure is employed to organize the classifiers, which begins with one classifier at the first layer and gradually refines the localization of feature points by more classifiers in the following layers. A Bayesian framework is configured for the inference of the feature points between the layers. The boosted classifiers detects facial features discriminately from its local neighborhood, while the inference between the layers constrains the searching space. Extensive experiments are reported to show its accuracy and robustness.

1 Introduction

Face alignment, whose objective is to localize the feature points on face images such as the contour points of eyes, noses, mouths and outlines, plays a fundamental role in many face processing tasks. The shape and texture of the feature points acquired by the alignment provide very helpful information for applications such as face recognition, modeling and synthesis. However, since the shape of the face may vary largely in practical images due to differences in age, expression and etc, a robust alignment algorithm, especially against errant initialization and face shape variation, is still a goal to achieve.

There have been many studies on face alignment in the recent decade, most of which were based on Active Shape Model (ASM) and Active Appearance Model (AAM), proposed by Cootes et al [1]. In all these improvements, local or global texture features are employed to guide an iterative optimization of label points under the constraint of a statistical shape model. Many different types of features such as Gabor[2], Haar wavelet[3], and machine learning methods such as Ada-Boosting[4, 5], k-NN[6] have been employed to replace the gradient

T.S. Huang et al. (Eds.): HCI/ECCV 2006, LNCS 3979, pp. 1–11, 2006.

feature and simple gaussian model in the classical ASM methods, improving the robustness of the texture feature. Besides, different methods of optimization such as weighted least-square[7, 8], statistical inference[9, 10] and optical flows[11] have been carried out to improve the efficiency of convergence.

However, most of these methods do not pay much attention to the initialization of the alignment, which strongly affects the performance of the alignment. As face detection algorithms only give a rough position of the face, it is often difficult to estimate all the feature points properly in initialization, especially for face images with expression and pose changes. With a bad initialization, the iterative optimization of both ASM and AAM will be stuck in local minima, and the alignment will fail.

To overcome this deficiency, we propose a novel method by building a hierarchical local texture classifier network, connecting face detection and face alignment into a smooth coarse-to-fine procedure. The algorithm is motivated by the following idea: since the texture patterns of feature points are often distinctive from their neighboring non-feature texture, localization of these feature textures can be considered as a pattern recognition task, like face detection task. Considering the face detection as the coarsest texture classifier at the first layer, a hierarchical structure can be settled to gradually refines the localization of feature points by more classifiers in the following layers. A Bayesian framework is configured for the inference of the feature points between the layers. Both the classifiers in different scales and the inter-layer inference are helpful for avoiding the local-minima problems.

There have been a previous work [5] trying to solve face alignment using face detection technique. Boosted classifiers, which have been widely used to recognize the face pattern, were introduced to recognize smaller texture patterns for every facial feature point. Compared with this work, our method not only employed boosted classifiers but also connect the face detection and alignment organically, further clarifying the coarse-to-fine relation between the two tasks.

There are also some other previous works employing hierarchical approaches. C.Liu et al.[10] introduced a hierarchical data driven Markov chain Monte Carlo (HDDMCMC) method to deduce the inter-layer correlation, while F. Jiao et al. [2] used Gabor wavelet in multi-frequency to characterize the texture feature. Many other methods used a multi-resolution strategy in their implementations, most of which simply take the alignment result in the low-resolution images as the initialization for high-resolution images. Compared with these methods, our method emphasizes both the inference of the inter-layer correlation and the local texture model, so as to achieve both robustness and efficiency.

The rest of the paper is organized as follows: In Section 2, classifiers based on boosted Haar-like feature are introduced to model the likelihood of feature texture patterns. In Section 3, hierarchical structure and algorithm of feature point selection are presented to organize these classifiers, and a Bayesian framework is configured for shape parameter inference between the layers. Extensive experiments are reported in Section 4. Finally, conclusions are drawn in Section 5.

2   Feature Texture Classifier

In order to localize the exact position of a feature point, its texture pattern should be modeled. Classical ASM method only uses a vector of gradient perpendicular to the contour to represent the feature, and characterizes it with Principle Component Analysis (PCA)[1]. Since this 1D profile feature and PCA are too simple, the localization can fall into local minima.

In our work, to make the local texture model more discriminative against non-feature texture patterns, we propose to learn the local texture classifiers by boosting weak classifiers based on Haar-like rectangle features. The boosted classifier is capable of capturing complicated texture pattern, such as human faces [12] and facial features[5]. Through Real AdaBoost learning [13], sample weights are adapted to select and combine weak classifiers into a strong one as,

$$conf(x) = \sum_{t=1}^{T} h_t(x) - b \qquad (1)$$

Thus, for each feature point i we will have a strong classifier $Conf_i(x)$. Given a feature pattern x, the strong classifier gives highly discriminative output values which can detect the corresponding feature point.

The classifiers can be trained to recognize facial feature texture in different scales from entire face to local patterns. And each classifier can be reinforced

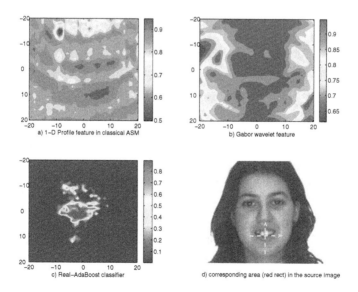

Fig. 1. (a),(b),(c) shows the confidence output of different methods around the feature point of lower-lip (crosspoint in (d)). the outputs in (c) are very discriminative between the ground truth position(center) and its neighborhood, while in (a) and (b) they are ambiguous.

by using a cascade of several classifiers [12]. For large pattern like entire face, an exhaustive searching on the image can find any possible candidate of the feature pattern by maximizing the likelihood output of the classifier. However, for localization of small patterns like facial feature, the large image space will make exhaustive searching time-consuming, and the output of classifiers would not be reliable in such large space. Hence, it is also important to constrain the searching space and maintain the geometry shape formed by the feature points, which we will discuss in Section 3.

3   Hierarchical Classifier Network

To connect the task of face detection and face alignment,let us consider them as two opposite bounds of a continuum (Fig.2). Shown on the left, the face detection task can explore large image space to find face regions. Its advantage is the high robustness against the complexity of background and the variation of face texture, while the detailed facial feature points are not aligned accurately. On the right, the face alignment task can localize each facial feature point accurately, given a good initialization. Inspired by the observation, we propose a coarse-to-fine structure combining the two tasks together to localize the facial shape starting from simple face detection rectangle.

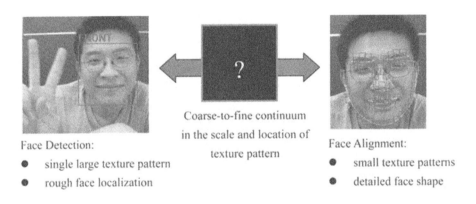

Coarse-to-fine continuum
in the scale and location of
texture pattern

Face Detection:
- single large texture pattern
- rough face localization

Face Alignment:
- small texture patterns
- detailed face shape

Fig. 2. Continuum of Face Detection and Face Alignment

3.1   Hierarchical Structure

The facial shape denoted by a vector $S^{(K)} = [x_1, y_1, \ldots, x_N, y_N]$, can be modeled by shape pose parameter p, q, as

$$S^{(K)} = T_q(\overline{S} + U \cdot p) \tag{2}$$

where p is the parameter of the point distribution model constructed by PCA with average shape $\overline{S}$ and eigenvectors U; $T_q(s)$ is the geometrical transformation based on 4 parameters: scale, rotation, and translation [1].

Given an image I as input, this coarse-to-fine procedure is illustrated in Fig.3: At the first layer, one single classifier is trained as a face detector to localize the central point (x_c, y_c), rotation angle θ and size W of the face. The face size is then normalized to L pixels in width, and p^0, q^0 are estimated through a MAP(max-a-posterior) inference,

$$\underset{p^0, q^0}{\arg\max} P(x_c, y_c, \theta, W | p, q) P(p^0) P(q^0) \qquad (3)$$

Then for the following layers, k^{th} layer for example, the further alignment task is divided into several sub-tasks localizing the feature points defined by point set $S^{(k)} = [x_i^{(k)}, y_i^{(k)}], i = 1..n_k$. And the geometry shape of $S^{(k)}$ is modeled by the parameters $p^{(k)}$ and $q^{(k)}$, as

$$S^{(k)} = A^{(k)} \cdot T_{q^{(k)}}(\overline{S} + U \cdot p^{(k)}) \qquad (4)$$

which represents the new feature points as a linear combination of original feature points using $A^{(k)}$.

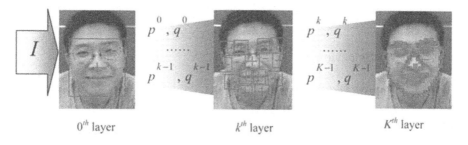

0th layer k^{th} layer K^{th} layer

0th**layer** $p^{(0)}, q^{(0)}$ are estimated from one classifier as a face detector;
k^{th}**layer** $p^{(k)}, q^{(k)}$ are estimated from both the local search and $p^{(k-1)}, q^{(k-1)}$;
K^{th}**layer** $p^{(K)}, q^{(K)}$ are estimated, localizing all the feature points in $S^{(K)}$.

0th**layer** $p^{(0)}, q^{(0)}$ are estimated from one classifier as a face detector;
k^{th}**layer** $p^{(k)}, q^{(k)}$ are estimated from both the local search and $p^{(k-1)}, q^{(k-1)}$;
K^{th}**layer** $p^{(K)}, q^{(K)}$ are estimated, localizing all the feature points in $S^{(K)}$.

Fig. 3. The hierarchical structure and coarse-to-fine procedure of face alignment

For each feature point in $S^{(k)}$ a classifier is trained with $\frac{L}{2^k} \times \frac{L}{2^k}$ sized rectangle features to distinguish the feature from non-feature. We can find each feature point independently by maximizing the corresponding likelihood output of the classifier. However, not only the likelihood of the texture but also the geometry shape of the feature points should be considered, and the feature point set should be constrained by the parameter of the shape model. Therefore, to align the face, the localization of the feature point set $S^{(k)}$ can be formulated by Bayesian inference given both the texture in this layer and the parameters estimated in the previous layer, which is

$$
\begin{aligned}
p^{(k)}, q^{(k)} &= \text{argmax}\, P(S^{(k)}|p^{(k-1)}, q^{(k-1)}, I^{(k)}) \\
&= \text{argmax}\, P(I^{(k)}|S^{(k)}, p^{(k-1)}, q^{(k-1)}) P(S^{(k)}|p^{(k-1)}, q^{(k-1)}) \\
&= \text{argmax}\, P(I^{(k)}|S^{(k)}) P(S^{(k)}|p^{(k-1)}, q^{(k-1)}) \\
&= \text{argmax}\, P(I^{(k)}|S^{(k)}) P(p^{(k-1)}, q^{(k-1)}|S^{(k)}) P(S^{(k)})
\end{aligned}
\tag{5}
$$

$P(I^{(k)}|S^{(k)})$ is the posterior probability of the feature texture, which can be acquired from the output of the classifiers; $P(p^{(k-1)}, q^{(k-1)}|S^{(k)})$ is the posterior probability of the parameters of previous layer.

Thus, the feature point set $S^{(k)}$ at k^{th} layer can be aligned by solving optimization (5). And the solution gives a prior distribution $P(S^{(k+1)}|p^{(k)}, q^{(k)})$ for the next layer, which will constrain its searching space of the feature points.

The localization and the inference repeat layer by layer, while the alignment result is refined gradually, until $S^{(K)}$ is localized in the last layer, which give the complete result of the alignment. There are two more factors to be further explained: 1) the selection of feature point sets and their geometry, which is how to get $S^{(1)}, S^{(2)}, \ldots S^{(K)}$ and $A^{(1)}, A^{(2)}, \ldots A^{(K)}$; 2) how to infer the shape and pose parameters using Eq.(5). We will introduce the two factors in Section 3.2, 3.3, respectively.

3.2   Feature Selection

Given the required feature point set $S^{(K)}$ for the final result of alignment, the feature point sets in other layers of the hierarchical structure are built from down to top. The selected feature points should minimize both the training error of the classifiers and the expectational error during the inference between the layers. Feature selection is a difficult problem, which could be done by exhaustive searching or other approximate algorithms such as Forward/Backward algorithms. To simplify the problem, in this paper, we use a heuristic algorithm based on prior-knowledge to give an approximate solution.

Instead of searching all possible feature point sets in the face region, we construct the feature point set of kth layer by merging the feature points in the $k + 1^{th}$ layer. The feature points from lower layer are merged only if they're close enough, in order that the texture patch of merged feature covers most of the patches before mergence. Denoting the feature point in the last layer as

$$
S^{(K)} = \{x_i^{(K)}, y_i^{(K)}|i = 1..n_K\}, \quad A_{i,j}^{(K)} = \begin{cases} 0 & : \quad i \neq j \\ 1 & : \quad i = j \end{cases}
\tag{6}
$$

And the width of the face shape is L. The algorithm for calculating feature point set $S^{(k)}$ and its geometry parameter $A^{(k)}$ is as follow:

Step 1. $F_i = \{(x_i^{k+1}, y_i^{k+1})\}, i = 1 \ldots n_{k+1}$;
Step 2. let $d(F_i, F_j) = \max\{\|(x, y) - (u, v)\| \,|\, (x, y) \in F_i, (u, v) \in F_j\}$,
   find $i^*, j^* = \underset{F_i, F_j \neq \emptyset, i \neq j}{\text{argmin}}\{d(F_i, F_j)\}$;

Step 3. If i^*, j^* exists, and $D_{min} < \frac{L/2^k}{2}$,
  let $F_{i^*} \leftarrow F_{i^*} \cup F_{j^*}$, $F_{j^*} \leftarrow \emptyset$, and goto Step.2
Step 4. Create one feature point for each nonempty F_i:

$$(x_i^k, y_i^k) \leftarrow \frac{1}{|F_i|} \sum_{(x_j, y_j) \in F_i} (x_j, y_j), \quad A^{(k)} \leftarrow \frac{1}{|F_i|} \sum_{(x_j, y_j) \in F_i} A_j^{(k+1)}$$

The hierarchical structure is constructed by applying the algorithm above from the $K - 1^{th}$ layer back to 0th layer. Fig.4 shows an example of 5 layers of a facial feature network. The feature patterns in different layers are from large to small representing more and more details of the facial features. The localization of features in lower layers can benefit from the estimation of facial shape in the upper layers through the Bayesian framework introduced in Section 3.1. The detail about the parameter inference will be presented in Section 3.3.

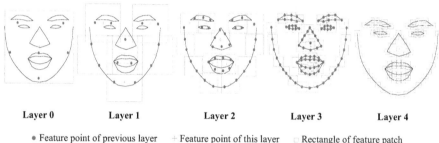

| Layer 0 | Layer 1 | Layer 2 | Layer 3 | Layer 4 |

• Feature point of previous layer   + Feature point of this layer   ▫ Rectangle of feature patch

Fig. 4. An example of 5-layer structure

3.3 Parameter Inference

In Section 3.1, the alignment at one specific layer is stated as a posterior estimation (MAP) given both the texture in this layer and the shape/pose parameters estimated in the previous layer, whose objective function is

$$\underset{p^{(k)}, q^{(k)}}{\arg\max} P(I^{(k)}|S^{(k)})P(p^{(k-1)}, q^{(k-1)}|S^{(k)})P(S^{(k)}) \tag{7}$$

The first two terms, which are respectively the likelihood of the patches $I^{(k)}$ and the likelihood of parameters $p^{(k-1)}, q^{(k-1)}$ given the feature points $S^{(k)}$, can be further decomposed into independent local likelihood functions of every feature point as $P(I^{(k)}|x_j^k, y_j^k)$ and $P(p^{(k-1)}, p^{(k-1)}|x_j^k, y_j^k)$. The third term, $P(S^{(k)})$, is the prior probabilistic distribution of the geometry shape, which we can get from the PCA analysis of out shape model[7].

By approximating these terms by Gaussians, the optimization problem in Eq.(7) can be restated as

$$\operatorname*{argmin}_{p^{(k)},q^{(k)}} \sigma_1 \sum_j \left\| \begin{bmatrix} x_j^k \\ y_j^k \end{bmatrix} - \begin{bmatrix} x_j' \\ y_j' \end{bmatrix} \right\|^2 + \sigma_2 \sum_j \left\| \begin{bmatrix} x_j^k \\ y_j^k \end{bmatrix} - \begin{bmatrix} x_j'' \\ y_j'' \end{bmatrix} \right\|^2 + \alpha \sum_j \left(\frac{p_j^{(k)}}{\lambda_j} \right)^2 \quad (8)$$

where (x_j, y_j) are modeled by parameters $p^{(k)}, q^{(k)}$, as

$$(x_j, y_j) = A_j^{(k)} \cdot T_{q^{(k)}} \left(\begin{bmatrix} \overline{x}_j \\ \overline{y}_j \end{bmatrix} + U_j \cdot p^{(k)} \right)$$

and (x_j', y_j') is location of the feature point maximizing the output of the jth feature classifier, as

$$(x_j', y_j') = \operatorname{argmax} \left\{ Conf_j^{(k)}(x_j', y_j') \right\}$$

and (x_j'', y_j'') is the expectational location derived from the shape model with $p^{(k-1)}, q^{(k-1)}$, as

$$(x_j'', y_j'') = A_j^{(k)} \cdot T_{q^{(k-1)}} \left(\begin{bmatrix} \overline{x}_j \\ \overline{y}_j \end{bmatrix} + U_j \cdot p^{(k-1)} \right)$$

(8) shows that the error cost of the jth feature point, could be explained as a weighted combination of the inconsistence in texture and shape respectively. The first term constrains the solution by the output of the classifier, while the second limits the searching space by the prior parameters. The weight σ_1 and σ_2 can be estimated from the outputs of the facial feature classifier $Conf_i(x, y)$ on this layer and previous layer.

(8) can be solved efficiently by a two-step or one-step minimum least square method, as discussed in [8]. Besides, since (x_j', y_j') will be estimated through a constrained local search, the optimization should also be calculated iteratively.

In summary, beginning with the location of the entire face texture, by doing the local search on different feature point sets and the parameter inference from layer to layer, the shape and pose parameters are optimized iteratively. The procedure ends at the last layer with the detail of the alignment result discovered.

4   Experiments

Experiments have been conducted on a very large data set consisting of 2,000 front face images including male and female aging from child to old people, many of which are with exaggerated expressions such as open mouths, closed eyes, or have ambiguous contours especially for old people. The average face size is about 180x180 pixels. We randomly chose 1,600 images for training, and the rest 400 images for testing. A 5-layer structure is implemented with normalized face rectangle at the first layer and 87 feature points at the last layer. Each of the facial feature classifiers is learned by AdaBoost combining 50 weak classifiers, except the one at the first layer for face detection. At the first layer, in order to achieve a high face detection rate, the face texture classifier is implemented in a nested cascade structure [14]. For comparison, classical ASM[1] and ASM with Gabor wavelet feature method [2], both with 3-layer pyramids, were implemented and trained on the same training set.

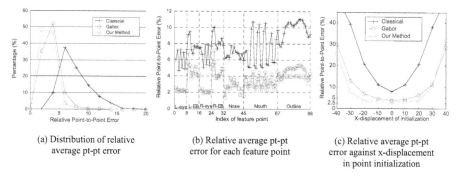

(a) Distribution of relative   (b) Relative average pt-pt   (c) Relative average pt-pt
average pt-pt error   error for each feature point   error against x-displacement
in point initialization

Fig. 5. Comparison of classical ASM, Gabor ASM and Our method

4.1   Accuracy

The accuracy is measured with relative pt-pt error, which is the point-to-point distance between the alignment result and the ground truth divided by the distance between two eyes. The distributions of the overall average error are compared in Fig.(5)(a). It shows that our method outperforms the other two. The average errors of the 87 feature points are compared separately in Fig.(5)(b). The x-coordinates, which represent the index of feature points, are grouped by organ. It also shows that the improvement of our methods is mainly on feature points of mouth and contour.

4.2   Robustness

To measure the robustness of our method, we initialized the face detection rectangle with a -40 to 40 displacements in x-coordinate. The variation of overall average error was calculated and shown in Fig.(5)(c). From the figure, we can see that our approach is more robust against bad initialization than the other two approaches.

Additional experiments on the subsets of the Purdue AR [15] and FERET [16] database are also carried out, of which the images bear large expression (closed eyes, big smiles, etc) and pose (about +/-30 rotation off-image-plane) variation. Those images are independent of the data set for training and testing. The experiment results show that our method is robust against the variations. And it should be mentioned that though the training set mainly focuses on frontal faces, our method can still deal with pose changes up to a domain so

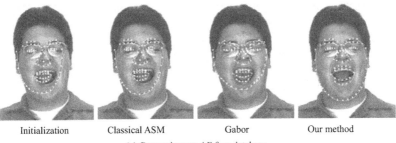

Initialization   Classical ASM   Gabor   Our method

(a) Comparison on AF face database

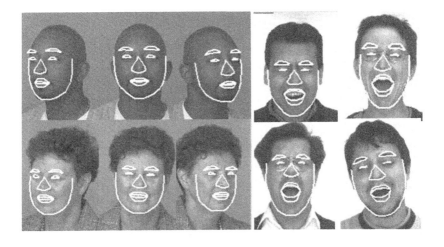

(b). Some results on face database of FERET (6 imgs on the left) and AR (4 imgs on the right)

Fig. 6. Additional experiment results

far as both eyes are visible, which is approximately +/-30 degrees. Some of the alignment results are shown in Fig.(6)(a)(b)(in which points are connected by line for clarity).

5   Conclusion

In this paper, We propose an automatic facial feature localization framework combining face detection and face alignment into a uniform coarse-to-fine procedure based on boosted classifier network. The boosted classifiers guarantee the facial features can be discriminated from its neighborhood even on faces with large expression variation and ambiguous contours, while the inter-layer inference efficiently constrains the searching space. Experiments show that our method is robust against changes in expression and pose.

Although our method is developed for the face alignment problem, it can also be applied to the localization of other deformable objects, especially ones with rich texture information. Further extension of our work will focus on the algorithm for the automatic feature selection, which should not be heuristic but learned from training data.

Acknowledgments

This work is supported mainly by a grant from OMRON Corporation. It is also supported in part by National Science Foundation of China under grant No.60332010.

References

1. Cootes, T.F., Taylor, C.J.: Statistical models of appearance for computer vision. Technical report, http://www.isbe.man.ac.uk/ bim/refs.html (2001)
2. Jiao, F., Li, S., Shum, H., Schuurmans, D.: Face alignment using statistical models and wavelet features. In: Proceedings of CVPR. (2003)
3. Zuo, F., de With, P.H.: Fast facial feature extraction using a deformable shape model with haar-wavelet based local texture attributes. In: ICIP. (2004)
4. Li, Y., Ito, W.: Shape parameter optimization for adaboosted active shape model. In: Proceedings of ICCV. (2005)
5. Zhang, L., Ai, H., Xin, S., Huang, C., Tsukiji, S., Lao, S.: Robust face alignment based on local texture classifers. In: Proceedings of ICIP. (2005)
6. van Ginneken, B., A.F.Frangi, J.J.Stall, ter Haar Romeny, B.: Active shape model segmentation with optimal features. IEEE-TMI (2002)
7. Yan, S., Li, M., Zhang, H., Cheng, Q.: Ranking prior likelihood distributions for bayesian shape localization framework. In: Proceedings of ICCV. (2003)
8. Hill, A., Cootes, T.F., Taylor, C.J.: Active shape models and the shape approximation problem. In: BMVC. (1995)
9. Zhou, Y., Zhang, W., Tang, X., Shum, H.: A bayesian mixture model for multi-view face alignment. In: Proceedings of CVPR. (2005)
10. Liu, C., Shum, H., Zhang, C.: Hierarchical shape modeling for automatic face localization. In: Proceedings of ECCV. (2002)
11. Matthews, I., Baker, S.: Active appearance models. IJCV (2004)
12. Viola, P., Jones, M.: Rapid object detection using a boosted cascade of simple features. In: Proceedings of CVPR. (2001) 511–518
13. Schapire, R.E., Singer, Y.: Improved boosting algorithms using confidence-rated predictions. Machine Learning 37 (1999) 297–336
14. Huang, C., Wu, B., Ai, H., Lao, S.: Omini-directional face detection based on real-adaboost. In: Proceedings of ICIP. (2004)
15. Martinez, A., Benavente, R.: The ar face database. cvc technical report no.24. Technical report (1998)
16. Phillips, P.J., Wechsler, H., Huang, J., Rauss, P.: The feret database and evaluation procedure for face recognition algorithms. Image and Vision Computing J (1998)

EigenExpress Approach in Recognition of Facial Expression Using GPU

Qi Wu, Mingli Song, Jiajun Bu, and Chun Chen

College of Computer Science, Zhejiang University,
Hangzhou, PR China, 310027
{wuqi, brooksong}@ieee.org,
{bjj, chenc}@zju.edu.cn

Abstract. The automatic recognition of facial expression presents a significant challenge to the pattern analysis and man-machine interaction research community. In this paper, a novel system is proposed to recognize human facial expressions based on the expression sketch. Firstly, facial expression sketch is extracted by an GPU-based real-time edge detection and sharpening algorithm from original gray image. Then, a statistical method, which is called *Eigenexpress*, is introduced to obtain the expression feature vectors for sketches. Finally, Modified Hausdorff distance(MHD) was used to perform the expression classification. In contrast to performing feature vector extraction from the gray image directly, the sketch based expression recognition reduces the feature vector's dimension first, which leads to a concise representation of the facial expression. Experiment shows our method is appreciable and convincible.

1 Introduction

Facial expression is one of the most powerful, natural, and immediate means for human beings to communicate their emotions and intentions, Relevant studies have been performed on the relationship between emotion and facial expressions since 1970s. Ekman[2, 3] grouped the facial expressions into six "universality" ones. Those are so called happiness, sadness, anger, fear, surprise, and disgust.

Some approaches[4] extract the facial features from the image, and these features are used as inputs into a classification system to categorize different facial expressions automatically. Some approaches[5] estimate the facial expression and the gender of a person based on statistical data analysis and neural classifiers. Also, Ekman's[2] introduced Facial Action Coding System(FACS)which codes the facial expressions by these facial feature components. However, there is much useless information around the expression features in the gray face images which influence the precision and efficiency of recognition.

Therefore, enhancing the edge between the components in the expression face will decrease the ambiguity and noise in the image. Consequently, it will emphasize the maximum feature components and reduce the redundant information. However it is known that the time cost of such operation is heavy on CPU.

T.S. Huang et al. (Eds.): HCI/ECCV 2006, LNCS 3979, pp. 12–20, 2006.

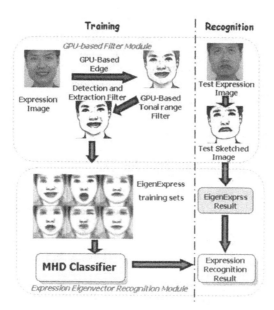

Fig. 1. System Overview

Recent development on computer graphics hardware makes GPU an extremely powerful graphics processing units (GPU). It can perform operations on very large amount of vectors very fast. It has more than one processing pipeline working in parallel. Also, the performance of GPU is growing at a high speed while Nvidia Corp. estimated that the Nvidia GeForce FX 7800 GPU performance peaks at 200 GigaFlops[10, 8]. Considering the parallel nature of implementing specific image processing with filters using vertex shader and pixel shader to process the image, this new graphics hardware is a suitable candidate for implementing them at an extremely high speed. This can be used to sharpen and detect the edge of the image of face expression to generate the corresponding sketch.

With the sketched images, the statistical based face representation, which we called *Eigenexpress*, is applied to represent them with serval eigenvectors that reserve the most energy of the images and set up the expression features training sets. Compared with the *Eigenfaces* [6], which plays a fundamental role and has been proved to be appreciable in face recognition, it is more robust and precise in facial expression recognition, especially for different people with different expressions. Finally, calculating the Modified Hausdorff distance between the test image's *Eigenexpress* representation and the seven basic expression training sets, the test expression eigenvectors, also generated from test expression images by GPU-base filter and Eigenexpress method, are classified into one of the seven basic categories. Figure 1. shows an overview of our facial expression recognition system with GPU-based filter which consists two parts: GPU-based facial feature extraction module, and expression recognition module.

2 GPU-Based Facial Feature Extraction

Modern graphics hardware give GPU a powerful capability to carry out Matrix-Vector operations. A series of filtering operations on image such as edge detection and sharpening, tone mapping, etc., can be performed at an extremely high speed. So it is suitable for GPU to implement such operations to obtain qualified sketched image at a very high speed.

In our GPU-based Edge Filter, each pixel in Gray-level Image can be operated concurrently under the stream pipeline of GPU.

Firstly, we convert it to luminance value $P_{i,j}$, $i \in Weight$, $j \in Height$ and sample all four around texture stages $P_{i,j}$, $P_{i+1,j}$, $P_{i,j+1}$, $P_{i+1,j+1}$.

Secondly, the two diagonal luminance differences of all four samples are computed, which Fig.2 shows to us,and we square each differences (it is easier and faster than obtaining its absolute value in GPU) ,then sum up them.

$$P'_{i,j} = (P_{i,j} - P_{i+1,j+1})^2 + (P_{i+1,j} - P_{i,j+1})^2 \qquad (1)$$

Thirdly, we multiply $P'_{i,j}$ with a large number δ to make the values visible.

$$P'_{i,j} = P'_{i,j} \cdot \delta \qquad (2)$$

Then, the result is subtract form 1 to invert edges black on white for we have normalize the gray range to $(0,1)$.

$$P'_{i,j} = 1 - P'_{i,j} \qquad (3)$$

Finally, we multiply edge-image with the luminance values and obtain the final result $P''_{i,j}$.

$$P''_{i,j} = P'_{i,j} \cdot P_{i,j} \qquad (4)$$

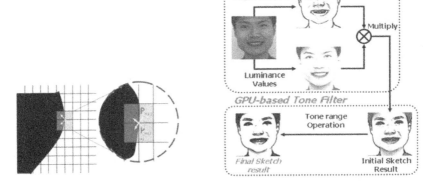

Fig. 2. Compute The Square Diagonal Luminance Differences

Fig. 3. Framework of GPU-based Filter

However, the result obtained from the method mentioned above still contains much noise make the image blurred and unreliable. So in our approach, a further step is taken to eliminate these high frequency noise by changing the tonal range, which can also be run extremely fast on GPU. For the world luminance L, it can be defined corresponding with the equation below [9].

$$TM(L) = LDMAX \frac{C(L) - C(L_{min})}{C(L_{max}) - C(L_{min})} \tag{5}$$

In our case, the mid-tone and the highlight are 0.25 and 175 respectively to compute L_{max} and L_{min}. As shown in Figure 3, we can see the luminance filtered sketch is cleaner than the initial one while keeping the detail of the face.

The following Figure 4. is one of our examples of creating the sketches corresponding to six basic expressions by the GPU-based filter which just takes 0.00153 second for each on average.

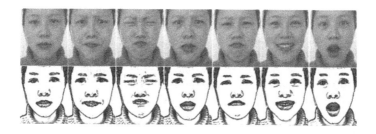

Fig. 4. Examples of sketched expressions

3   Facial Expression Recognition

As an important human behavior for conveying psychological information, facial expression has been studied for some ten's of years in different modal: visual, speech, etc. But there is still much work need to be done to get a higher accuracy. Similar to the previous work, we also categorize given face images into seven classifications: neutral, happy, anger, surprise, disgust, sad and fear.

3.1   EigenExpress Method

The way of EigenExpress uses the Karhunen-Loeve Transform (KLT)[12] for the representation of face expressions. Once a set of eigenvectors is computed from the ensemble face covariance matrix, a facial expression image can be approximately reconstructed using a weighted combination of the eigenvectors, called EigenExpress, The weights that characterize the expansion of the given image in terms of eigenvectors constitute the feature vector. When a new test image is given, the weights are computed by projecting the image onto the vectors. The classification is then carried out by comparing the distances between the weight vectors of the test image and the images from the training sets.

To implement the EigenExpress, assuming F_i is a column vector of dimension N^2 representation of a sample facial expression image with the mean face computed as $\boldsymbol{m_p} = 1/M \sum_{i=1}^{M} F_i$, where M is the number of training samples, Removing the mean face from each training image, we have $P_i = F_i - \boldsymbol{m_p}$. The training set the form an N^2 by M matrix $A_p = [P_1, P_2, \cdots, P_M]$. We can find the orthogonal eigenvectors u_n corresponding to the C-largest eigenvalues λ_n of matrix $A_P^T A_P$

$$(A_P^T A_P)u_n = \lambda_n u_n \quad (n = 0, 1, \cdots, C - 1) \tag{6}$$

In order to reduce the dimension of the matrix $A_P^T A_P$ which is N^2 by N^2 to decrease the computational complexity, we want to use M instead of N^2. Therefore, We use dominant eigenvector estimation method [11] multiplying both sides by A_P and we have

$$(A_P A_P^T)A_P u_n = A_P \lambda_n u_n \tag{7}$$

The orthonormal eigenvector matrix of the covariance matrix is

$$u_n = A_P u_n \lambda_n^{-1/2} \tag{8}$$

For a new facial expression image P_k, its projection coefficients in the eigenvector space form the vector $b_P = u_P^T P_k$ which is used as a feature vector for the classification. We call this feature vector *Eigenexpress*.

Because of the structural similarity across all face images, strong correlation exists among facial expression images. The *Eigenexpress* method takes advantage of such a high correlation to produce a highly compressed representation of facial expression images, thus improves expression recognition more efficiently.

3.2 Modified Hausdorff Distance

Hausdorff distance[14, 13] is a robust method to describe the similarity between two point sets. Given two finite point sets $A = \{a_1, a_2, \cdots, a_p\}$ and $B = \{b_1, b_2, \cdots, b_q\}$, The Hausdorff distance is defined as

$$H(A, B) = max(h(A, B), h(B, A)) \tag{9}$$

where

$$\begin{cases} h(A, B) = \max_{a \in A} \min_{b \in B} \| a - b \| \\ h(B, A) = \max_{b \in B} \min_{a \in A} \| b - a \| \end{cases} \tag{10}$$

And $\|\|$ is some underlying norm on the points of A and B (e.g., the L_2 or Euclideam norm).

The function $h(A, B)$ is called the directed Hausdorff distance from A to B. That is, $h(A, B)$ in effect ranks each point a_i of A based on its distance $\| a_i - b_j \|$ to the nearest point b_j of B and then used the largest distance as the value of $h(A, B)$. The Hausdorff distance $H(A, B)$ is the maximun of $h(A, B)$ and $h(B, A)$. Thus, it measures the degree of maximum mismatch between two sets.

In our approach, For both the gray based and sketch based facial expression recognition, we compute the the the basic expression mean face's *Eigenexpress* first, which is represented as b_{P_m}, $m = [1, .., 7]$. Then we compare b_P with b_{P_m} by Modified Hausdorff Distance(MHD) which defines:

$$H_{LK}(b_P, b_{P_m}) = \max(h_L(b_P, b_{P_m}), h_K(b_{P_m}, b_P))$$ (11)

where,

$$\begin{cases} h_K(b_{P_m}, b_P) & = \frac{1}{N_{b_{P_m}}} \sum_{b \in b_{P_m}} \min_{a \in b_P} \| a - b \| \\ h_L(b_P, b_{P_m}) & = \frac{1}{N_{b_P}} \sum_{a \in b_P} \min_{b \in b_{P_m}} \| b - a \| \end{cases}$$ (12)

where $N_{b_{P_m}}$ and N_{b_P} are the number of eigenvectors in Eigenexpress sets b_{P_m} and b_P.

The Hausdorff distance for recognition is different for the seven basic *Eigenexpress*. It determines which basic expression the test image should belong to.

Compared with basic Hausdorff distance, MHD is not sensitive to the noise and ambiguity of the image. It can decrease the influence of irrelevant eigenvectors and make more precise and robust classification.

4   Experiment and Evaluation

In our approach, GPU-based filter is used to preprocess facial images in performing the recognition. In this way, noise and redundant information in the image are reduced, and all the component such as eyes, mouth and chin which have obvious differences in seven basic expressions will be enhanced.

As for the *Eigenexpress*-based method, after expression sketching preprocessing, because the feature components have been enhanced, most of the energy concentrate on the top eigenvectors by which we can use much less eigenvectors to keep the same energy as before. Consequently, it reduces computing workload and makes the expression recognition more efficient.

In order to build a model that is flexible enough to cover most of the typical variation of face, we have collected more than 840 gray expression images form 40 people with different basic expressions and their corresponding sketched expression images processed by our GPU-based filter as the data sets.

Then we select 280 gray expression images which is $200 * 200$ pixels do the comparison. Table 1 shows the method's performance on the gray image, while Table 2 gives out a higher accuracy on the sketched image. We use Confusion matrix of the emotion recognition. (Columns represent the emotion elected by our method for samples belonging to the emotion of each row)

In our experiment, the most clearly recognizable expression is Surprise and Happy which have great difference form others, but Anger and Disgust are a bit lower with their difficulty for recognition not only by our method but also by human beings.

The comparison of recognition accuracy in different methods(PCA + Neural Network, ASM + SVM, Eigenexpress in Gray and Eigenexpress in Sketch)are

Table 1. Gray-level Image Based Expression Recognition with *Eigenexpress*

	Anger	Disgust	Fear	Neutral	Sad	Joy	Surprise	Tot	Ratio.
Anger	30	4	1	3	2	0	0	40	75%
Disgust	1	21	3	4	7	0	4	40	52.5%
Fear	1	4	27	3	0	2	3	40	67.5%
Neutral	1	3	3	27	4	0	2	40	67.5%
Sad	2	1	6	5	25	1	0	40	62.5%
Happy	0	0	1	3	0	34	2	40	85%
Surprise	0	1	3	0	0	2	34	40	85%
Total	35	34	44	45	38	39	45	280	70.71%

Table 2. Sketch Image Based Expression Recognition with *Eigenexpress*

	Anger	Disgust	Fear	Neutral	Sad	Joy	Surprise	Tot	Ratio.
Anger	32	2	3	2	1	0	0	40	80%
Disgust	2	31	2	2	2	0	1	40	77.5%
Fear	1	2	33	2	0	0	2	40	82.5%
Neutral	2	0	2	34	1	1	0	40	85%
Sad	0	1	1	1	37	0	0	40	92.5%
Happy	0	0	0	1	0	38	1	40	95%
Surprise	0	0	0	0	0	1	39	40	97.5%
Total	37	36	41	42	41	40	43	280	87.14%

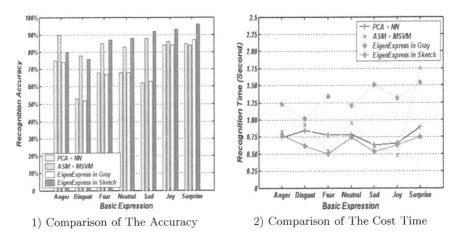

1) Comparison of The Accuracy   2) Comparison of The Cost Time

Fig. 5. Comparison between previous methods and our method

listed in Fig.5(1). It is obvious from the figures that our method has the highest accuracy than any others, and the significant improvements (almost 27.13% compared to PCA+NN, 4.7% compared to ASM+MSVM and 28.34% compared to Eigenexpress in Gray) are obtained by using Eigenexpress in Sketch generated by GPU. However, it is also clear from the comparison of the recognition cost time in Fig.5(2) that the using of GPU in our method improves the recognition speed greatly(almost 11.52% compared to PCA+NN, 34.2% compared to ASM+MSVM and 15.43% compared to Eigenexpress in Gray).

5 Conclusion

The automatic recognition of facial expression presents a significant challenge to the pattern analysis research community because the expression is generated by nonrigid object deformations vary from person to person. The expression recognition from a static image is, particularly, a more difficult problem compared to the recognition from an image sequence[15] due to lack of information during expression actions. In this paper, we propose a novel GPU enhanced facial expression recognition which use GPU-based filter to preprocess and convert the gray expression image to sketched facial expression at extremely high speed. *Eigenexpress* is introduced to analyze the features of different basic expressions to set up training sets. Finally, we use Modified Hausdorff distance to classify the expression images into seven basic expressions. Experiment result shows sketch based approach can obtain better result not only on the recognition accuracy but also the time cost.

In future work, more detailed work and complex action units will be considered in our system. Our goal is to find a way which can acquire a better effect with getting higher recognition accuracy and speeding less recognition time. we will employ new way to track the facial expression features more precisely and quickly. In addition, the combination of facial expression recognition and speech recognition will make our system more efficient and accurate.

Acknowledgments

This work is supported by National Science Foundation China 60203013 and Key Technologies R&D Program of Zhejiang Province (2004C11052 & 2005C23047).

References

1. Maja.Pantic and Leon J.M.Rothkrantz. Automatic analysis of facial expression: *The state of the art.*. IEEE Transactions on Pattern Analysis and Machine Intelligence, 22(12):1424-1445,2000
2. P. Ekman, W.V. Friesen, *Facial Action Coding System: Investigator's Guide.* Consulting Psychologists Press, 1978.
3. P.Ekman, *Strong Evidence for Universals in Facial Expressions: A Reply to Russel's Mistaken Critique.* Psychological Bulletin, 115(2):268-287, 1994.
4. Ira Cohen, Nicu Sebe, Fabio G. Cozman, Marcelo C. Cirelo, Thomas S. Huang, *Learning Bayesian Network Classifiers for Facial Expression Recognition with both Labeled and Unlabeled data*IEEE Conference on Computer Vision and Pattern Recognition, pp.595-602, 2003.

5. T.Wilhelm, A.Backhaus, *Statistical and Neural Methods for Vision-based Analysis of Facial Expressions and Gender*. IEEE International Conference on Systems, Man and Cybernetics, Vol. 3, pp.2203-2208. 2004.
6. M. Turk and A. Pentland, *Eigenfaces for Recognition*, Journal of Cognitive Neuroscience, 3(1):71-86, 1991
7. M. Macedonia, *The Gpu Enters Computing's Mainstream* IEEE Computer, October 2003.
8. Jens Krüger and Rüdiger Westermann, *Linear Algebra Operators for GPU Implementation of Numerical Algorithms* ACM Siggraph 2003, pp. 908-916.
9. Michael Ashikhmin: *A Tone Mapping Algorithm for High Contrast Images*. Eurographics Workshop on Rendering (2002) 1–11
10. NVIDIA Corporation, *Industry's Premiere Game Developers Proclaim NVIDIA GeForce 7800 GTX GPUs Platform of Choice for Next-Generation Game Development*. 2005.
11. K.Fukunaga, *Introduction to Statistical Pattern Recognition*, New York: Academic, 1972.
12. M.Kirby and L.Sirovich, *Application of the karhunen-loeve procedure for the characterization of human faces*, IEEE Transaction on Pattern Analysis and Machine Intelligence, Vol.12, pp.103-108, 1990.
13. D.P. Huttenlocher, G. A. Klanderman and W.J. Rucklidge. *Comparing images using the Hausdorff distance*, In IEEE Trans. PAMI, Vol. 15, No. 9, 1993 9.
14. W.J. Rucklidge. *Efficient Visual Recognition Using the Hausdorff Distance*. Springer-Verlag, 1996.
15. Mingli Song, Jiajun Bu, Chun Chen, *Expression Recognition from Video using A Coupled Hidden Markov Model*, IEEE TENCON'2004, 2004.

Face Representation Method Using Pixel-to-Vertex Map (PVM) for 3D Model Based Face Recognition

Taehwa Hong[1], Hagbae Kim[1], Hyeonjoon Moon[2], Yongguk Kim[2],
Jongweon Lee[2], and Seungbin Moon[2]

[1] Department of Electrical and Electronic Engineering,
Yonsei University, Seoul, Korea
{riccati, hbkim}@yonsei.ac.kr
[2] School of Computer Engineering,
Sejong University, Seoul, Korea
{hmoon, ykim, jwlee, sbmoon}@sejong.ac.kr

Abstract. 3D model based approach for face recognition has been spotlighted as a robust solution under variant conditions of pose and illumination. Since a generative 3D face model consists of a large number of vertices, a 3D model based face recognition system is generally inefficient in computation time. In this paper, we propose a novel 3D face representation algorithm to reduce the number of vertices and optimize its computation time. Finally, we evaluate the performance of proposed algorithm with the Korean face database collected using a stereo-camera based 3D face capturing device.

1 Introduction

Face recognition technology can be used in wide range of applications such as identity authentication, access control, and surveillance system. A face recognition system should be able to deal with various changes in face images. However, the variations between the images of the same face due to illumination and head pose are almost always larger than image variation due to change in face identity.

Traditional face recognition systems have primarily relied on 2D images. However, they tend to give a higher degree of recognition performance only when images are of good quality and the acquisition process can be tightly controlled.

Recently, many literatures on 3D based face recognition have been published with various methods and experiments. It has several advantages over traditional 2D face recognition: First, 3D data provides absolute geometrical shape and size information of a face. Additionally, face recognition using 3D data is more robust to pose and posture changes since the model can be rotated to any arbitrary position. Also, 3D face recognition can be less sensitive to illumination since it does not solely depend on pixel intensity for calculating facial similarity. Finally, it provides automatic face segmentation information since the background is typically not synthesized in the reconstruction process [1].

Recently, V. Blanz, T. Vetter and S. Romdhani [2][3][4] proposed a method using 3D morphable model for face recognition robust to pose and illumination. They

T.S. Huang et al. (Eds.): HCI/ECCV 2006, LNCS 3979, pp. 21–28, 2006.

constructed a 3D morphable model with 3D faces acquired from a 3D laser-scanner, which are positioned in well calibrated cylindrical coordinates. Especially, texture information of 3D face is well defined in the reference frame where one pixel corresponds to one 3D vertex perfectly. Thereafter, they found appropriate shape and texture coefficient vectors of the model by fitting it to an input face using Stochastic Newton Optimization (SNO)[3] or Inverse Compositional Image Alignment (ICIA)[4][5] as a fitting algorithm and then evaluated the face recognition performance of with well-known databases such as PIE[6] and FERET[7]. However, this approach has complexity and inefficiency problems caused by very large vertex number (about 80,000 ~ 110,000) despite of excellent performance.

In this paper we propose a novel 3D face representation algorithm based on pixel-to-vertex map (PVM). It is possible to reduce the vertex number of each 3D face remarkably and all the 3D faces can be aligned with correspondence information based on the vertex number of a reference face simultaneously.

This paper is organized as follows. The next section presents the proposed algorithm for 3D face representation. Section 3 simply describes the procedure of fitting the 3D model to an input image. Experimental results are presented in Section 4 based on a Korean database. Finally, conclusions and future work are discussed in Section 5.

2   3D Face Representation

In general, a 3D face scan consists of texture intensity in 2D frame and geometrical shape in 3D. Especially, the shape information is represented by close connections of many vertices and polygons. Since the vertex number of each of 3D face scans is different from each other, it is necessary to manipulate them to have the same number of vertices for consistent mathematical expression.

We propose a novel 3D face representation algorithm for vertex number correspondence, which is performed by masking, PVM and alignment as showed in Fig. 1.

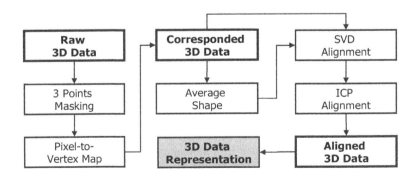

Fig. 1. 3D face representation process

2.1 Vertex Correspondence Using the Pixel-to-Vertex Map (PVM)

In the first place, we have registered three fiducial points manually, which are left eye center, right eye center and mouth center (from the 2D texture information of each 3D face scan). Thereafter, a fixed point for each of three fiducial points is set in texture frame. Each fiducial point of 3D face scans is located in the same position of the texture frame. Then, a face region is separated from the background by adopting an elliptical mask.

Pixel-to-vertex map (PVM) is a sort of binary image, which classifies pixels in the masked face region into ones mapped to a vertex and the opposite. We call the former active pixel (AP) and the latter inactive pixel (IP). A PVM example is shown in Fig. 2.

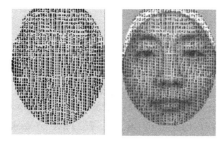

Fig. 2. An example showing pixel-to-vertex map (PVM). AP and IP are expressed as dark and bright pixel in an elliptical mask, respectively.

The procedures for the vertex correspondence using PVM are as follows:

- Construct each PVM matrix of M+1 3D face scans and build the vertex position matrix by stacking the position vector of the vertex mapping to each AP in a PVM. If the resolution of the texture frame is C by R, the PVM matrix of the ith scan, denoted by $\mathbf{M}_i$ and the vertex position matrix of the ith scan, denoted by $\mathbf{P}_i$ are obtained as

$$\mathbf{M}_i = \begin{bmatrix} m_{11}^i & m_{12}^i & \cdots & m_{1C}^i \\ m_{21}^i & & & \\ \vdots & & \ddots & \vdots \\ m_{R1}^i & & \cdots & m_{RC}^i \end{bmatrix}, \qquad m_{rc} = \begin{cases} 0, \text{ if } \mathrm{p}_{rc} \text{ is IP} \\ 1, \text{ if } \mathrm{p}_{rc} \text{ is AP} \end{cases}. \tag{1}$$

$$\mathbf{P}_i = [\mathbf{v}_1^i \quad \mathbf{v}_2^i \quad \cdots \quad \mathbf{v}_{s(\mathbf{M}_i)}^i]. \tag{2}$$

where p_{rc} is the pixel positioned at (r, c) in the texture frame and $s(\mathbf{M}_j)$ is size of the PVM, the number of the APs in the PVM. Also, $\mathbf{v}_j^i = [x_j \ y_j \ z_j]^T$ is the 3D position vector of the vertex mapping to the jth AP in the ith scan.

- Select a reference pixel-to-vertex map(RPVM), denoted by $\mathbf{M}^R$, by maximizing this criterion.

$$\mathbf{M}^R = \arg \max_{\mathbf{M}_j} s(\mathbf{M}_j). \tag{3}$$

The size of the RVPM, $s(\mathbf{M}^R)$ means the vertex number of a reduced subset. Then, all scans will be in correspondence with the vertex number. Likewise, the vertex position matrix of RVMP are denoted by $\mathbf{P}^R$.

- Compute each modified vertex position matrix of all scans except one selected for the RPVM.

$$\hat{\mathbf{v}}_k^i = \begin{cases} \mathbf{v}_{p(k)}^i, & \text{if } \mathrm{m}_{p(k)}^i \text{ is AP} \\ \mathbf{v}^N, & \text{if } \mathrm{m}_{p(k)}^i \text{ is IP} \end{cases}. \tag{4}$$

$$\mathbf{v}^N = \sum_{q=1}^{8} w_q \mathbf{v}_q. \tag{5}$$

where $\hat{\mathbf{v}}_k^i$ is a modified vertex position vector, which is the same to the position of the original vertex if mapped to AP, otherwise should be acquired by an interpolation method. And, the subscripted $p(k)$ means the position of the pixel mapped to the vertex related to kth column in the $\mathbf{P}^R$. We have to seek an appropriate 3D position $\mathbf{v}^N$ for a vertex mapped to IP using linear combinations of the positions of vertices mapped to 8 nearest neighbor APs in the PVM of the target scan as defined in eq. (5).

2.2 Face Alignment and Model Generation

Through the PVM presented in previous subsection, it is possible that all 3D face scans in our database (See Section 4) are expressed with the same number of vertex points. To construct a more accurate model, it is necessary to utilize some techniques for face alignment, which is transforming the geometrical factors (scale, rotation angles and displacements) of a target face based on a reference face. Face alignment in our research is achieved by adopting singular value decomposition (SVD)[8] and Iterative Closest Points (ICP)[9][10] sequentially.

We constructed separate models from shapes and textures of 100 Korean people by applying PCA[11][12] independently. The separate models are generated by linear combination of the shapes and textures as given by eq. (6).

$$\mathbf{S} = \mathbf{S}_0 + \sum_{j=1}^{N_S} \alpha_j \mathbf{S}_j, \qquad \mathbf{T} = \mathbf{T}_0 + \sum_{j=1}^{N_T} \beta_j \mathbf{T}_j. \tag{6}$$

where $\boldsymbol{\alpha} = [\alpha_1 \, \alpha_2 \cdots \alpha_{N_S}]$ and $\boldsymbol{\beta} = [\beta_1 \, \beta_2 \cdots \beta_{N_T}]$ are the shape and texture coefficient vectors (should be estimated by a fitting procedure). Also, $\mathbf{S}_0$ and $\mathbf{S}_j$ are the shape average model and the eigenvector associated with the jth largest eigenvalue of the shape covariance matrix, $\mathbf{T}_0$ and $\mathbf{T}_j$ in textures likewise.

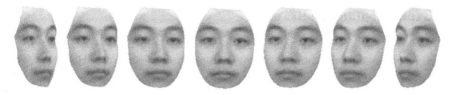

Fig. 3. A generative 3D model. These are rotated versions of the 3D model in Y-axis direction. Each version from the first is ranged from -45 degrees to 45 degrees at 15 degrees interval.

3 Fitting the 3D Model to a 2D Image

Shape and texture coefficients of the generative 3D model are estimated by fitting it to a given input face. This is performed iteratively as close as possible to the input face. Fitting algorithms, called stochastic Newton optimization (SNO) and inverse compositional image alignment (ICIA) were utilized in [3] and [4], respectively. It is generally accepted that SNO is more accurate but computationally expensive and ICIA is less accurate but more efficient in computation time[4].

We also explore the ICIA algorithm as a fitting method to guarantee the computational efficiency. Given an input image, initial coefficients of shape and texture and projection parameters for the model are selected appropriately. Initial coefficients of shape and texture usually have zero values but projection parameters are manually decided by the registration of some important features. Then, fitting steps are iterated until convergence to a given threshold value, minimizing the texture difference between the projected model image and the input image. During the fitting process, texture coefficients are updated without an additive algorithm at each iteration. But in case of shape coefficients, their updated values are not acquired with ease because of the nonlinear problem of structure from motion (SFM) [13]. To solve it, we recover the shape coefficients using SVD based global approach [14] after the convergence.

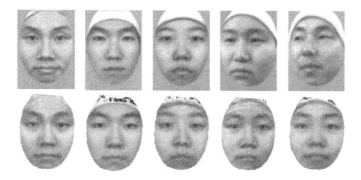

Fig. 4. Fitting results. The images in top row are input images and those in bottom row are the fitted versions of our 3D model. Especially, the inputs to the third column are frontal and the others are rotated 30 degrees approximately.

4 Experimental Results

We evaluate our face recognition system based on a 3D model generated using proposed representation algorithm. As mentioned in previous sections, 3D Korean faces are collected using a Geometrix Facevision 200, which is a stereo-camera based capturing device offering a 3D face scan including approximately 30,000 ~ 40,000 vertices and corresponding 2D texture image. There are 218 3D face scans collected from 110 people during 3 sessions, which are limited with frontal views and neutral expressions, in our database. We used 100 scans in session 1 for 3D model generation and 52 scans in other sessions for the performance evaluation. Also, 7 sided face images with range from 15 to 40 degrees are acquired separately using the same device for variant pose test. Some example scans are showed in Fig. 4.

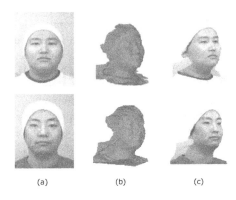

      (a)   (b)   (c)

Fig. 5. 3D face examples: (a) texture images (b) shaded shapes (c) rendered 3D views

The experimental results to frontal and sided faces are shown in Table 1. In both experiments, we utilized the L2 norm and angle combined with Mahalanobis distance as a distance metric, denoted by L2+ Mahalanobis and Angle+ Mahalanobis respectively [15]. Also, we performed additional experiments on two cases, one is to use only texture coefficients and the other is to combine texture and shape coefficients. Recognition accuracy with rank 1 in both tests was 90.4% (47 out of 52 subjects) and 85.7% (6 out of 7 subjects) respectively. The average fitting time taken without the shape recovery was 3.7s on 1.73GHz Pentium-M and 1GB RAM, but when the recovery process is included, it required 11.2s on the same machine. A remarkable

Table 1. Recognition accuracy with rank 1 to frontal faces and pose variant faces

	Only Texture		Texture + Shape	
	L2+Mah	L2+Angle	L2+Mah	L2+Angle
Frontal faces	90.4%	86.5%	90.4%	88.5%
Pose variant faces	71.4%	85.7%	71.4%	85.7%
Computation time	3.7s		11.2s	

result is that utilizing the shape coefficients doesn't improve the performance meaningfully in spite of increased computation time.

5   Conclusion

In this paper, we presented a novel 3D face representation algorithm for 3D model based face recognition system. On the basis of the presented method, an original 3D face scan including 30,000 ~ 40,000 vertices could be represented with about 5,000 vertices based on PVM. We have generated 3D morphable model using 100 3D face images (each 3D face image composed of 4822 vertices). Then, shape and texture coefficients of the model were estimated by fitting into an input face using the ICIA algorithm. For 3D model generation and performance evaluation, we have made the Korean 3D face database from a stereo-camera based device. Experimental results show that face recognition system using the proposed representation method is more efficient in computation time. Romdhani et. al. [4] presented that the fitting time takes about 30 seconds with almost same condition as our proposed algorithm, though it is less accurate in terms of recognition performance. Our future works will focus on automatic initialization in the fitting procedure.

Acknowledgement

This research was performed for the Promotion and Support Program of Strategic Industry Innovation Cluster, one of the Collaboration Programs for Industry, Academy and Research Institute funded by City of Seoul, Korea.

References

1. T. Papatheodorou and D. Rueckert. Evaluation of 3D Face Recognition Using Registration and PCA. AVBPA 2005, LNCS 3546, pp. 997-1009, 2005.
2. V. Blanz and T. Vetter. A Morphable Model for the Synthesis of 3D Faces. In Computer Graphics, Annual Conference Series(SIGGRAPH), pp. 187-194, 1999.
3. V. Blanz and T. Vetter. Face Recognition Based on Fitting a 3D Morphable Model. IEEE Transactions on Pattern Analysis and Machine Intelligence. 25(9):1063-1074, 2003.
4. S. Romdhani and T. Vetter. Efficient, Robust and Accurate Fitting of a 3D Morphable Model. In IEEE International Conference on Computer Vision, 2003.
5. S. Baker and I. Matthews. Equivalence and Efficiency of Image Alignment Algorithms. In CVPR, 2001.
6. T. Sim, S. Baker and M. Bsat. The CMU Pose, Illumination, and Expression Database. IEEE Transactions on Pattern Analysis and Machine Intelligence. 25(12):1615-1618, 2003.
7. P. Phillips, H. Moon and P. Rauss. The FERET Evaluation Methodology for Face Recognition Algorithms. IEEE Transactions on Pattern Analysis and Machine Intelligence, 22(10):1090-1104, 2000.
8. B. K. P. Horn, H. M. Hilden and S. Negahdaripour. Closed-Form Solution of Absolute Orientation Using Orthonormal Matrices. Journal of the Optical Society of America A, vol. 5, pp. 1127-1135, 1988.

9. P. J. Besl and N. D. Mckay. A Method for Registration of 3D Shapes. IEEE Transactions on Pattern Analysis and Machine Intelligence, 14(2):239-256, 1992.
10. X. Lu, A. Jain and D. Colbry. Matching 2.5D Face Scans to 3D Models. IEEE Transactions on Pattern Analysis and Machine Intelligence, 28(1):31-43, 2006.
11. M. Turk and A. Pentland. Eigenfaces for recognition. J. Cognitive Neuroscience, vol. 3, pp.71-86, 1991.
12. T. Vetter and T. Poggio. Linear Object Classes and Image Synthesis from a Single Example Image. IEEE Transactions on Pattern Analysis and machine Intelligence, 19(7):733-742, 1997.
13. B. Bascle and A. Blake. Separability of pose and expression in facial tracking and animation. In Sixth International Conference on Computer Vision. pp. 323-328. 1998.
14. S. Romdhani, N. Canterakis, and T. Vetter. Selective vs. Global Recovery of Rigid and Non-rigid Motion. Technical report, CS Dept., Univ. of Basel, 2003.
15. H. Moon and P. Phillips. Computational and Performance Aspects of PCA-Based Face-Recognition Algorithms. Perception. Vol. 30. pp. 303-321, 2001.

Robust Head Tracking with Particles Based on Multiple Cues Fusion

Yuan Li[1], Haizhou Ai[1], Chang Huang[1], and Shihong Lao[2]

[1] Department of Computer Science, Tsinghua University Beijing, China
[2] Sensing and Control Technology Lab, OMRON Corporation, Kyoto, Japan
ahz@mail.tsinghua.edu.cn

Abstract. This paper presents a fully automatic and highly robust head tracking algorithm based on the latest advances in real-time multi-view face detection techniques and multiple cues fusion under particle filter framework. Visual cues designed for general object tracking problem hardly suffice for robust head tracking under diverse or even severe circumstances, making it a necessity to utilize higher level information which is object-specific. To this end we introduce a *vector-boosted multi-view face detector*[2] as the "face cue" in addition to two other general visual cues targeting the entire head, color spatiogram[3] and contour gradient. Data fusion is done by an *extended particle filter* which supports multiple distinct yet interrelated state vectors (referring to face and head in our tracking context). Furthermore, pose information provided by the face cue is exploited to help achieve improved accuracy and efficiency in the fusion. Experiments show that our algorithm is highly robust against target position, size and pose change as well as unfavorable conditions such as occlusion, poor illumination and cluttered background.

1 Introduction

Visual object tracking has long been a topic that attracts much research interest due to its crucial value in applications including human-computer interaction, robotics, visual surveillance, etc. In particular, human head tracking is one of its most popular cases. Although head tracking is commonly used as experiment scenario to evaluate general tracking algorithm, due to lack of strong object-specific information (observation model) general tracking algorithms are not robust and often require manual initialization, therefore cannot meet the requirements of many practical problems which are confronted with large variation of both target appearance and enrivonment.

Traditional approaches concerning human head/face tracking mainly fall into two classes by how specialized their visual cues are: 1) those which rely on general information such as color, corner points, edge, background substraction, etc[13][12][4][11], and 2) those which involves sophisticated geometry and texture models[14][15][16].

Most approaches from the first class can actually be applied to any objects other than head/face. Although their generality allow for certain degree of variability of the target and the scene, without any object-specific knowledge their

T.S. Huang et al. (Eds.): HCI/ECCV 2006, LNCS 3979, pp. 29–39, 2006.

discriminant power between target and clutter is often in peril under tough conditions such as bad illumination and strong background noise.

On the other hand, approaches from the second class are mainly designed for facial feature tracking, but can hardly fit into our head tracking problem since they require a relatively clear appearance and limited view change of the target, both of which ensure the information needed to support complicated models.

The above discrepancy reflects two difficulties fettering the solution of head tracking problem, which we attempt to overcome in this paper:

- **The lack of prior knowledge of the type of object being tracked.** The incapability of general visual cues to capture the characteristics of a given type of target can be compensated by statistical learning. Therefore, in addition to two general cues based on color and gradient, we further adopt a vector-boosted real-time multi-view face detector which is trained over large data sets. It provides a strong visual cue by inferring face occurrence from image patches.
- **The fusion difficulty induced by information asymmetry between head rear and face.** Face is a distinct pattern and provides plenty information (e.g. the layout and appearance of facial organs) for specialized modeling. On the contrary, the head, especially the head rear, involves much larger appearance variability, and provides no relatively strong and stable features. If we want to seek aid from both highly specialized prior knowledge of face and general visual cues for the head, such asymmetry must be reconciled in the data fusion step. Here we extend the popular probabilistic tracking tool – particle filter – to support both the face state and the head state, taking into account their statistical interrelationship.

The rest of this paper is organized as follows. Section 2 introduces the face detector, defines the face state vector and describes how to construct a probabilistic observation model of face. Section 3 defines the head state vector and presents two complementary observation models based on color spatiogram and contour gradient. Section 4 addresses the fusion problem of multiple observation models with multiple distinct but interrelated state vectors, and proposes the extended particle filter. Section 5 gives the experimental results and Section 6 reaches the conclusion.

2   Face-Based Observation Model

Face is the most characteristic feature of human head. Despite its possible invisibility during the out-of-plane rotation of head, face can still be a strong aid to head tracking if the visual attributes of face are captured and discriminated against non-face appearance. However, in conventional face/head tracking, face detection is only performed as initialization due to its computational cost. As a representative of the few attempts in integrating detection into tracking, [5] adopted the detector of [9] to achieve successful face tracking, but its speed was far from real-time. In fact, although much effort has been paid on face detection[10][9][7][2], it is until recent years that face detection algorithms which meet the real-time and multi-view requirements of head tracking are developed[7][2]. Here we adopt a vector-boosted tree structure detector for multi-view face[2] to construct an probabilistic observation model for tracking. The detector covers a range of $\pm90°$ out-of-plane rotation (yaw) and $\pm45°$ in-plane rotation (tilt). In the following, we briefly introduce the detector and describe how to model the output of the detector into a observation likelihood.

2.1   Vector-Boosted Multi-view Face Detector

For multi-view face detection, the detector accomplishes two tasks at one time: to distinguish faces and non-faces and to distinguish different poses. A width-first-search tree structure is used to balance these two aspects as well as to enhance the detector in both accuracy and speed(Fig. 1). Each node of the tree is a strong classifier boosted from numerous weak classifiers, and it decides whether an input image patch should be rejected or passed to one or more of its son nodes. In one detection run, an image patch starts from the root node and travels along tree paths by width-first search, and is accepted as face if and only if it passes one or more leaf-node.

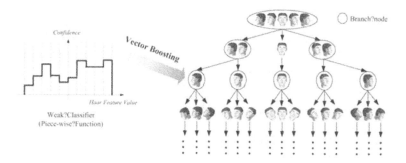

Fig. 1. Weak classifier and the tree structure face detector

To train branch nodes which are responsible for not only rejecting non-faces but also identifying poses, the Vector Boosting algorithm is extended from the Real AdaBoost. For the weak classifier we use haar-like feature[7] and piece-wise function (Fig. 1, left) which is proved in several works[8][2] to be a more effective substitute for traditional threshold-type function.

2.2   Face Likelihood

For the face likelihood $p(\mathbf{y}^{face}|\mathbf{x}^f)$ we define the face state vector as $\mathbf{x}^f = \langle x^f, y^f, s \rangle$, where $\langle x^f, y^f \rangle$ denotes the center coordinates of face square region, and s denotes the side length of the square.

Face detector focuses on whether an input image patch is a face or not, but now we are interested in how likely it is a face $(p(\mathbf{y}^{face}|\mathbf{x}^f))$, which is rarely discussed in existing works. Here we propose a probabilistic approximation of $p(\mathbf{y}^{face}|\mathbf{x}^f)$ from boosted classifiers by diving further into the training process.

For any given state $\mathbf{x}^f$, the corresponding image patch I_x is input to the tree-structured detector. The face likelihood can be formulated as

$$p(\mathbf{y}^{face}|\mathbf{x}^f) = p(face|I_x) = \frac{p(I_x|face)p(face)}{p(I_x)}$$

$$= \frac{r \cdot p(I_x|face)}{r \cdot p(I_x|face) + p(I_x|\overline{face})} \tag{1}$$

where $p(face|I_x)$ is the probability of the image patch I_x being a face, and $r = p(face)/p(\overline{face})$ is the a priori ratio. To compute Eq. (1) we need to estimate $p(I_x|face)$, $p(I_x|\overline{face})$, and r.

Given I_x, a strong classifier (tree node) v projects it to some feature space and outputs a confidence $f_v(I_x)$, and $p(I_x|face)$ and $p(I_x|\overline{face})$ are well approximated by $p(f_v(I_x)|face)$ and $p(f_v(I_x)|\overline{face})$ respectively. The latter two is adequately estimated by two single gaussian distribution learned from training samples on which v is trained.

On the other hand, every strong classifier's a priori ratio between face and non-face is also different, since the face and non-face subspaces have been continually refined by its ancestor classifiers – in training this refinement corresponds to the reselection of training samples: samples that have been rejected by ancestor nodes are no longer included. Typically, every strong classifier has a certain non-face sample rejecting rate and face sample accepting rate, so that if we assume an initial face/non-face a priori ratio r_0 for the root node, the a priori ratio r_v for any other nodes v can also be computed by

$$r_v = r_0 \prod_{i=0}^{l-1} \frac{\alpha_{v_i}}{1 - \beta_{v_i}} \tag{2}$$

where $\{v_0, ..., v_{l-1}\}$ is the path from root node v_0 to v, and α_{v_i} and β_{v_i} are the face sample accepting rate and non-face sample rejecting rate of v_i respectively.

Therefore,

$$p(\mathbf{y}^{face}|\mathbf{x}^f) \doteq \frac{r_v \cdot p(f_v(I_x)|face)}{r_v \cdot p(f_v(I_x)|face) + p(f_v(I_x)|\overline{face})} \tag{3}$$

where we choose v as the node with the maximum layer number among all nodes that I_x have passed.

3   Head-Based Observation Model

To accomplish head tracking with full range out-of-plane rotation, we further introduce two relatively general image cues targeting the head as a whole: one is the color spatiogram[3] of head region, and the other is intensity gradient along head contour. Both of them are based on the elliptical head state vector defined as $\mathbf{x}^h = \langle x^h, y^h, a, b \rangle$, where $\langle x^h, y^h \rangle$ denotes the center coordinates of the head ellipse, a and b denote the semimajor axis and semiminor axis respectively.

3.1 Color Spatiogram

Compared with color histogram which discard all spacial infomation, a spatiogram models each bin by the mean and covariance of the locations of pixels that contribute to that bin. The color space of our spatiogram consists of B-G, G-R and R+B+G, which are divided into N_1, N_2 and N_3 different values respectively. We denote the spatiogram as $\mathbf{h} = (h_1, h_2, ..., h_N)$, $N = N_1 N_2 N_3$, with each bin $h_i = \langle n_i, \mu_i, \Sigma_i \rangle$, where n_i is portional to the number of pixels that belongs to the ith bin, and is normalized so that $\sum_{i=1}^{N} n_i = 1$, and μ_i and Σ_i are the mean vector and covariance matrix of the coordinates of the pixels.

To obtain the color likelihood of a candidate state of the target, the spatiogram of the candidate is compared to a reference spatiogram. We do this by extending the widely-used distance metric of traditional histogram[12] to spatiogram and propose a color likelihood model that differs from [3].

Regard a spatiogram as a weighed gaussian mixture (each bin of a spatiogram as a gaussian distribution $N(\mu_i, \Sigma_i)$ with the weight n_i), the Bhattacharyya coefficient can be derived as:

$$\rho = \sum_{i=1}^{N} \left(\sqrt{n_{i,1} n_{i,2}} \sqrt{\frac{|\Sigma_{i,1}|^{\frac{1}{2}} |\Sigma_{i,2}|^{\frac{1}{2}}}{|\bar{\Sigma}_i|}} \exp\left(-\frac{1}{8} \hat{\mu}_i^T \bar{\Sigma}_i^{-1} \hat{\mu}_i\right) \right) \tag{4}$$

where $\bar{\Sigma}_i = \frac{\Sigma_{i,1} + \Sigma_{i,2}}{2}$, and $\hat{\mu}_i = \mu_{i,2} - \mu_{i,1}$. The distance between $\mathbf{h}_1$ and $\mathbf{h}_2$ can be computed as

$$D(\mathbf{h}_1, \mathbf{h}_2) = (1 - \rho)^{1/2} \tag{5}$$

And by assuming that the squared distance is exponentially distributed as in [12], the color likelihood model is

$$p(\mathbf{y}^{color} | \mathbf{x}^h) \propto \exp\left(-D^2(\mathbf{h_x}, \mathbf{h}_{ref})/2\sigma_{color}^2\right) \tag{6}$$

(a) Original frame   (b) By color histogram   (c) By color spatiogram

Fig. 2. Comparison between likelihood maps given by (b)color histogram and (c)color spatiogram. The reference is obtained from the man's head region in (a). The spatiogram better distinguishes the tracking target (the man) from the woman.

Compared with traditional histogram, color spatiogram contains a richer description of the target(Fig. 2), and therefore can increase the robustness in tracking as long as the tracked object's spatial color distribution remains relatively stable. On the other side, however, spatiogram is also more vulnerable to dramatic variability of spatial color distribution – which is the exact case in head tracking, since the target exhibits different appearance under different poses. Fortunately, this drawback is solved gracefully by fusing the pose information given by the face model to construct one reference spatiogram for each pose respectively, and updating these references from time to time.

3.2   Contour Gradient

As a complementary counterpart of object color, gradient information has been used in head tracking by accumulating intensity gradient along the contour[11], and by modeling the occurrence of edge points along contour normals by Poisson distribution[1]. The latter is better formulated in probabilistic sense, but also requires a more accurate contour curve. In practice we use a combination of the two for our elliptical contour state.

For any given head state x^h, a certain number of points on the contour curve is uniformly sampled and the normal at each point is searched within a finite length L for the maximum gradient magnitude. Let $g(x^h)$ denote the sum of the maximum along each normal, and the gradient likelihood is modeled by a gaussian-like function with the form

$$p(y^{grad}|x^h) \propto \exp\left(-\frac{(g_{max} - g(x^h))^2}{2\sigma^2_{grad}}\right) \tag{7}$$

where $g_{max} = \max_{x^h}\{g(x^h)\}$ is the maximum gradient sum among all calculated candidate states.

4   Multiple Cues Fusion by Extended Particle Filter

4.1   Standard Particle Filter

Particle filter[1] is a well-known tracking technique based on Bayesian sequential estimation. Denote the state of the target object and the observation at time t by x_t and y_t respectively, the filtering distribution $p(x_t|Y_t)$ stands for the distribution of target state given all observations $Y_t = (y_1, ..., y_t)$ up to time t. This filtering distribution can be computed by the famous two-step recursion

$$\text{Prediction}: p(x_t|Y_{t-1}) = \int p(x_t|x_{t-1})p(x_{t-1}|Y_{t-1})dx_{t-1}$$
$$\text{Update}: p(x_t|Y_t) \propto p(y_t|x_t)p(x_t|Y_{t-1}) \tag{8}$$

The recursion requires a dynamic model $p(x_t|x_{t-1})$ and an observation model $p(y_t|x_t)$, and is initialized with the distribution of initial state $p(x_0)$. To handle non-gaussian distributions which lead to analytical intractability, particle filter[1] approximates the two steps by a set of weighed samples $\{x_t^{(i)}, \pi_t^{(i)}\}_{i=1}^N$.

Such probabilistic approach provides a neat way to fuse multiple observation models. In most of existing literature, these observation models either share the same state vector or work on state vectors that form a strict hierarchy[4]. In contrast, our head tracking system involves observation models targeting two distinct yet interrelated state vectors: the face $\mathbf{x}^f$ and the head $\mathbf{x}^h$. In the next section we show that they can be fused by some well-modeled sampling process.

4.2   Extending Particle Filter to Multiple Interrelated States

Since head is the object of interest while face is not always present in the tracking process, we make the target state of the filter $\mathbf{x}_t = \mathbf{x}_t^h$, and make $\mathbf{x}_t^f$ an auxiliary state. The observation vector $\mathbf{y}_t$ is $\langle \mathbf{y}^{color}, \mathbf{y}^{grad}, \mathbf{y}^{face} \rangle$.

Assuming independency among different observation models, the unified observation likelihood can be formulated as (suppressing the time index t for compactness)

$$p(\mathbf{y}|\mathbf{x}) = p(\mathbf{y}^{color}|\mathbf{x}^h)p(\mathbf{y}^{grad}|\mathbf{x}^h)p(\mathbf{y}^{face}|\mathbf{x}^h) \tag{9}$$

Note that the observation $\mathbf{y}^{face}$ can only be obtained based on the auxiliary state $\mathbf{x}^f$. And yet the state $\mathbf{x}^f$ and $\mathbf{x}^h$ are interrelated, meaning that given the position and size of head, the position and size of the corresponding face obey some distribution $p(\mathbf{x}^f|\mathbf{x}^h)$. Therefore,

$$p(\mathbf{y}|\mathbf{x}) = p(\mathbf{y}^{color}|\mathbf{x}^h)p(\mathbf{y}^{grad}|\mathbf{x}^h)\int p(\mathbf{y}^{face}|\mathbf{x}^f)p(\mathbf{x}^f|\mathbf{x}^h)d\mathbf{x}^f \tag{10}$$

Inspired by the idea of standard particle filter, the integral part in Eq. (10) can also be computed by sampling, resulting in the extended particle filter algorithm used in our system shown in Table 1.

Table 1. Intermediary Sampling Particle Filter

With $\{\mathbf{x}_{t-1}^{(i)}, \pi_{t-1}^{(i)}\}_{i=1}^N$ the particle set at the previous time step, proceed as follows at time t:

- Resample: simulate $\alpha_i \sim \{\pi_{t-1}^{(i)}\}_{i=1}^N$, and replace $\{\mathbf{x}_{t-1}^{(i)}, \pi_{t-1}^{(i)}\}_{i=1}^N$ with $\{\mathbf{x}_{t-1}^{(\alpha_i)}, 1/N\}_{i=1}^N$
- Prediction: simulate $\mathbf{x}_t^{(i)} \sim p(\mathbf{x}_t|\mathbf{x}_{t-1}^{(i)})$
- For each $\mathbf{x}_t^{(i)}$, compute two parts of its weight respectively:
  - Using the head contour (gradient and color) cue:
    $\pi_t^{head,(i)} = p(\mathbf{y}_t^{color}|\mathbf{x}_t^{(i)})p(\mathbf{y}_t^{grad}|\mathbf{x}_t^{(i)})$
  - Using the face cue:
    Simulate $\{\mathbf{x}^{f,(j)}\}_{j=1}^M \sim p(\mathbf{x}^f|\mathbf{x}_t^{(i)})$
    $\pi_t^{face,(i)} = \sum_{j=1}^M p(\mathbf{y}_t^{face}|\mathbf{x}^{f,(j)})$
- If $\sum_{i=1}^N \pi_t^{face,(i)} > \Gamma$ (Γ is a constant threshold decided empirically),
    Face visible, for each $i = 1..N$: $\pi_t^{(i)} = \pi_t^{head,(i)}\pi_t^{face,(i)}$
  Else
    Face invisible, for each $i = 1..N$: $\pi_t^{(i)} = \pi_t^{head,(i)}$
- Normalize weight so that $\sum_{i=1}^N \pi_t^{(i)} = 1$

Until now the only problem we have left out is the distribution $p(\mathbf{x}^f|\mathbf{x}^h)$ representing the interrelation between the two state vectors, which varies as pose changes(Fig. 3), so it is desirable that this distribution be modelled separately for different poses. In practice, we use five offline-learned gaussian models for left/right full profile, left/right half profile and frontal respectively. Thanks to the pose information provided by the face cue, we online select the model for sampling.

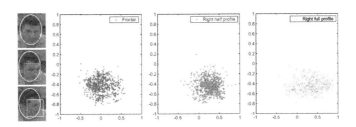

Fig. 3. Interrelation of face state and head state. Positions of face center relative to head center for different poses are shown (left: frontal, middle: right half profile, right: right full profile). Head center is at the origin and head region is scaled to $[-1, 1] \times [-1, 1]$.

5   Experimental Results

In implementation, full frame face detection is performed for auto-initialization. Once a face is detected, the neighboring region is searched for an optimal head contour and the initial particle set is obtained by gaussian random sampling. Zero-order dynamic model is used in the filtering process.

Quantitative Analysis. We collected three video data sets for evaluation. The first is a collection of movie clips (50 clips, 11,424 frames), the second contains video clips shot by desktop "webcam" and test data used in [3](10 clips, 3,156 frames), and the third contains family video clips shot by hand-hold video camera(23 clips, 17,916 frames). Two trackers are tested, ours and another which adopts color histogram and contour gradient cues fused by standard particle filter (we did not use color spatiogram for comparison because we have found that without any pose information, color spatiogram performs even worse than histogram due to large variation of target spacial color distribution caused by pose or illumination change in the test data, as we have analyzed at the end of Section 3.1).

Table 2 shows the success rate of both methods. The success rate is the proportion of frames successfully tracked. To obtain this rate, the tracking result is compared to the manually labeled ground truth (one out of every 12 frames). The criterion of successful tracking is: the center of the bounding rectangle of output head region must be inside the ground truth head rectangle, and the area should be within $[0.5, 1.5]$ times of that of the ground truth rectangle.

Table 2. Comparison of success rate over different data sets

Algorithm	Movie Data Set	Webcam Data Set	Family Video Data Set
Ours	87.18%	91.63%	83.39 %
Color & Gradient	69.64%	68.44%	46.54%

(a) Different poses and cluttered background

(b) Unbalanced illumination and drastic motion

(c) Occlusion in cluttered background

(d) Crowded scene

Fig. 4. Examples of tracking results

Scenario Analysis. Our test data sets include various challenging cases. See Fig. 4 for a few examples, where both head contour and face position and pose are shown.

Time Analysis. Our tracker runs at about 15 to 18 frames per second on a laptop with a Pentium M740(1.73MHz) CPU and 512M RAM, for videos of size 320 × 240 (including video acquisition and playing results online). For a comparison, the speed of frame-based detection using the same multi-view face detector is about 8 to 10 frames per second. Temporal filtering has largely reduced the load of detection, achieving higher efficiency.

6   Conclusion

We have presented an approach to integrate the latest technique in real-time multi-view face detection and two general visual cues into the probabilistic tracking framework for robust head tracking. By modeling the output of the vector-boosted tree structure detector into a probabilistic face likelihood, our approach is able to utilize high level prior knowledge of the tracking target and hence can handle much harder cases. To fuse the specialized face cue and the general head cues, the standard particle filter is extended to support both the face state and the head state, which are different but interrelated.

The resulting head tracker is experimented in various kinds of video sequences and shows versatility under different unfavorable circumstances. We believe our algorithm can be easily extended to the multi-object case (for example, by combining the multi-modal particle filter proposed by [17]), and the appearance of new target can be gracefully handled by the detector. Further research can also be done on statistical learning of the head pattern and online updating detectors.

Acknowledgments

This work is supported mainly by a grant from OMRON Corporation. It is also supported in part by National Science Foundation of China under grant No.60332010.

References

1. Isard, M., Blake, A.: Condensation – conditional density propagation for visual tracking. IJCV **28(1)** (1998) 5–28
2. Huang, C., Ai, H., Li, Y., Lao, S.: Vector boosting for rotation invariant multi-view face detection. In: ICCV. (2005)
3. Birchfield, S., Rangarajan, S.: Spatiograms versus histograms for region-based tracking. In: CVPR. (2005)
4. Perez, P., Vermaak, J., Blake, A.: Data fusion for visual tracking with particles. Proceedings of IEEE (issue on State Estimation) (2004)
5. Verma, R.C., Schmid, C., Mikolajczyk, K.: Face detection and tracking in a video by propagating detection probabilities. PAMI **25(10)** (2003) 1215–1228
6. Okuma, K., Taleghani, A., D., F., Little, J.J., Lowe, D.G.: A boosted particle filter: Multitarget detection and tracking. In: ECCV. (2004)
7. Viola, P., Jones, M.: Robust real-time object detection. In: IEEE Workshop on Statistical and Theories of Computer Vision. (2001)

8. Wu, B., Ai, H., Huang, C., Lao, S.: Fast rotation invariant multi-view face detection based on real adaboost. In: Intl. Conf. on Automatic Face and Gesture Recognition. (2004)

9. Schneiderman, H., Kanade, T.: A statistical to 3d object detection applied to faces and cars. In: CVPR. (2000)

10. Rowley, H.A.: Neural Network-based Human Face Detection. PhD thesis, Carnegie Mellon University (1999)

11. Birchfield, S.: Elliptical head tracking using intensity gradients and color histograms. In: CVPR. (1998)

12. Comaniciu, D., Ramesh, V., Meer, P.: Real-time tracking of non-rigid objects using mean shift. In: CVPR. (2000)

13. Perez, P., Hue, C., Vermaak, J., Gangnet, M.: Color-based probabilistic tracking. In: ECCV. (2002)

14. Matthews, I., Baker, S.: Active appearance models revisited. Technical Report CMU-RI-TR-03-02, The Robotics Institute, Carnegie Mellon University (2002)

15. Cootes, T.F., Edwards, G.J., Taylor, C.J.: Active appearance models. PAMI **23(6)** (2001) 681–684

16. Cascia, M.L., Sclaroff, S., Athitsos, V.: Fast, reliable head tracking under varying illumination: An approach based on registration of texture-mapped 3d models. PAMI **22(4)** (2000) 322–336

17. Vermaak, J., Doucet, A., Perez, P.: Maintaining multi-modality through mixture tracking. In: ICCV. (2003)

Vision-Based Interpretation of Hand Gestures for Remote Control of a Computer Mouse

Antonis A. Argyros and Manolis I.A. Lourakis

Institute of Computer Science,
Foundation for Research and Technology - Hellas (FORTH),
Vassilika Vouton, P.O.Box 1385, GR 711 10,
Heraklion, Crete, Greece
{argyros, lourakis}@ics.forth.gr
http://www.ics.forth.gr/cvrl/

Abstract. This paper presents a vision-based interface for controlling a computer mouse via 2D and 3D hand gestures. The proposed interface builds upon our previous work that permits the detection and tracking of multiple hands that can move freely in the field of view of a potentially moving camera system. Dependable hand tracking, combined with fingertip detection, facilitates the definition of simple and, therefore, robustly interpretable vocabularies of hand gestures that are subsequently used to enable a human operator convey control information to a computer system. Two such vocabularies are defined, implemented and validated. The first one depends only on 2D hand tracking results while the second also makes use of 3D information. As confirmed by several experiments, the proposed interface achieves accurate mouse positioning, smooth cursor movement and reliable recognition of gestures activating button events. Owing to these properties, our interface can be used as a virtual mouse for controlling any Windows application.

1   Introduction

Being simpler and more intuitive compared to typing at a command prompt, the WIMP (Windows, Icons, Menus and Pointing devices) paradigm dominates most modern graphical user interfaces (GUIs) [12]. WIMP represents an interaction style according to which the user communicates with a computer by means of a pointing device (e.g., mouse, trackball, stylus, etc), that is used to select commands from drop-down menus or icons on the display screen that correspond to predefined actions. In its most common application, the WIMP paradigm demands the user to make physical contact with the pointing device to convey his input. This requirement imposes constraints that, in certain situations, render working with a computer uncomfortable. Such difficulties are emphasized further by the increasing ubiquity of computing power and the continuous downsizing of computer hardware.

In recent years, research efforts seeking to provide more natural, human-centered means of interacting with computers have gained growing interest. A

T.S. Huang et al. (Eds.): HCI/ECCV 2006, LNCS 3979, pp. 40–51, 2006.

particularly important direction is that of *perceptive user interfaces*, where the computer is endowed with perceptive capabilities that allow it to acquire both implicit and explicit information about the user and the environment. Vision has the potential of carrying a wealth of information in a non-intrusive manner and at a low cost, therefore it constitutes a very attractive sensing modality for developing perceptive user interfaces. Proposed approaches for vision-driven interactive user interfaces resort to technologies such as head tracking, face and facial expression recognition, eye tracking and gesture recognition. A detailed review of existing methods and applications is given in [9]. Due to our interest in systems supporting direct, natural interaction with GUI components, below we limit discussion to such systems only. Zhang et al [14], for instance, propose a vision-based gesture interface system which employs an arbitrary quadrangle-shaped planar object (e.g., an ordinary piece of paper) and a tip pointer (e.g., a fingertip) as an intuitive, mobile input device. Corso et al [5] detect simple visual interaction cues that provide more complex interaction capabilities when sequenced together. Their system supports direct interaction with interface components through actions and gestures. Robertson et al [10] rely on monocular hand tracking and gesture recognition to control an intelligent kiosk. Malik and Laszlo [8] describe a system that supports two-handed, multi-finger gestural interaction by relying on a stereo vision system that estimates finger orientations and fingertip 3D positions.

In this paper, we describe a vision-based approach towards providing a remote, non-contact mouse control interface. This perceptive interface employs standard web-cameras with robust vision techniques and allows the user's hands to subsume the hardware pointing devices in the framework of the WIMP paradigm. Our vision algorithms are fast enough to operate at high video rates on commodity hardware, thus ensuring unhampered interactivity. Two different variants of mouse control interfaces have been investigated. The first makes use of 2D information regarding detected and tracked hands and is based on a single-camera system. The second makes use of 3D information regarding the detected and tracked hands and requires stereoscopic input. Both interfaces have been extensively tested in several real-world situations and the experience we gained from these user trials is presented in detail.

The rest of the paper is organized as follows. Section 2 provides a description of the vision techniques giving rise to the perceptual input on which the proposed gesture-based mouse control interface is built. Section 3 describes the two developed mouse control interfaces. Section 4 presents experimental evidence on the accuracy and the usability of the developed interfaces followed by a critique on the advantages and disadvantages of each of them. Finally, section 5, summarizes the paper by providing the main conclusions from this work.

2   From Images to Gestures

The proposed approach to gesture-based human-computer interaction is based on our previous work on 2D and 3D tracking of multiple skin colored objects. In the following sections, we provide a brief overview of that work. More detailed presentations can be found in [1, 2].

2.1   The 2D Hand Tracker

Our 2D tracker supports tracking of multiple blobs exhibiting certain color distributions in images acquired by a possibly moving camera. The tracker encompasses a collection of techniques that enable the detection and the modeling of the blobs possessing the desired color distribution(s), as well as their temporal association across image sequences. Hands, corresponding to skin-colored blobs, are detected with a Bayesian classifier which is bootstrapped with a small set of training data. Then, an on-line iterative training procedure is employed to refine the classifier using additional training images. On-line adaptation of color probabilities is used to enable the classifier to cope with illumination changes.

Tracking over time is realized through a scheme which can handle multiple targets that may move in complex trajectories, occlude each other in the field of view of a possibly moving camera and whose number may vary over time. Briefly, tracking operates as follows. At each time instant, the camera acquires an image on which the appropriately colored blobs (i.e. connected sets of skin-colored pixels) are detected. A set of hand hypotheses that have been tracked up to the current time instant is also being maintained. The detected hands are then associated with the existing hand hypotheses. The goal of this association is twofold: first, to assign a new, unique label to each new hand that enters the field of view of the camera for the first time; and second, to propagate in time the labels of already detected hands. The tracker has the ability to dynamically adapt to skin color distribution variations that are caused by illumination changes. Furthermore, its prototype implementation on a conventional Pentium IV processor at 2.5 GHz operates on 320×240 live video in real time (30Hz). It is worth pointing out that this performance is determined by the maximum acquisition frame rate that is supported by our IEEE 1394 camera, rather than the latency introduced by the computational overhead for tracking hands.

2.2   3D Hand Tracking and Reconstruction

The 3D hand tracker employs a stereoscopic camera system that delivers two synchronized video streams. Each of these streams is processed by an instance of the previously described 2D hand tracker. In order to achieve 3D reconstruction of the hand positions and hand contours (i.e. silhouettes), correspondence of hand blobs between stereo images needs to be established. We formulate this problem as an instance of the *stable marriage problem*. The two sets from which elements to be paired are selected, correspond to the sets of hands detected and tracked in the two images of the stereo pair. According to the original formulation of the stable marriage problem, the two sets whose elements are paired have equal cardinalities. In our case, this might not hold due to the different numbers of hands detected and tracked in each of the stereo images. For this reason, we have extended [6] to handle the case of sets with unequal cardinalities. The required preferences among the members of sets are formed by employing the epipolar constraint [13] on their centroids. Specifically, the better the centroids of the hands satisfy the epipolar constraint, the higher their mutual preference becomes.

The algorithm described above matches hands between the synchronous images of a stereo pair. To be able to recover the 3D contour of a particular hand, point-wise correspondences of contour pixels are also required. The lack of texture in the images of hands and the presence of considerable depth discontinuities are conditions that do not favor correlation-based approaches towards solving the correspondence problem. Instead, we compute correspondences through a top-down approach in which the basic idea is that if two matching hand contours can be aligned, then the necessary correspondences for 3D reconstruction can easily be extracted. To perform this type of alignment, we employ a robust variant of the Iterative Closest Point (ICP) algorithm [3]. Several robust variants of the ICP algorithm have been proposed that can solve the problem in the presence of measurement outliers and, possibly, shape defects. In our hand tracking scenario, such outliers and shape defects can be due to inaccuracies in skin color detection. Filtering them out is very important because it safeguards the later process of 3D reconstruction against gross errors due to erroneous point matches. The robust variant of ICP that we employ is similar in spirit with the one described in [4]; the major difference is that we use the Least Median of Squares (LMedS) robust estimator [11] in all steps of the general ICP algorithm, instead of the Least Trimmed Squares (LTS) estimator of [4]. The initial contour alignment that is necessary for bootstrapping the ICP algorithm is easily achieved by exploiting orientation information already available to the 2D hand tracker [2].

To recover 3D coordinates, camera calibration parameters along with point correspondences (either matched hand centroids or matched hand contour points) serve as input to a triangulation technique. A typical problem with triangulation relates to the fact that noise in 2D points combined with calibration inaccuracies often result in making skew the back-projected 3D lines defined by the camera optical centers and the corresponding image points. This problem is dealt with by reconstructing each 3D point as the midpoint of the minimal length straight line segment whose endpoints lie on the skew back-projected lines [7].

The developed method for binocular hand tracking and 3D reconstruction has served as a building block in a number of diverse applications and has been tested extensively in various environments. One particular application concerns a cognitive vision system whose goal is the automatic interpretation of the activities of people handling tools. Figures 1(a),(b) show a stereo pair from a related experiment in which a person operates a CD player while a pair of cameras is observing the scene. Detected skin-colored pixels are illustrated in white. The contour of the hand is delineated in light blue. Figure 1(c) shows the trajectory of the centroid of the hand as this was computed by the proposed system. As it can be verified from this figure, the hand moves towards the CD player, opens the tray, moves towards the CD, picks up the CD, puts it on the open tray, closes the tray and retracts to its rest position. For improving the readability of the 3D

44   A.A. Argyros and M.I.A. Lourakis

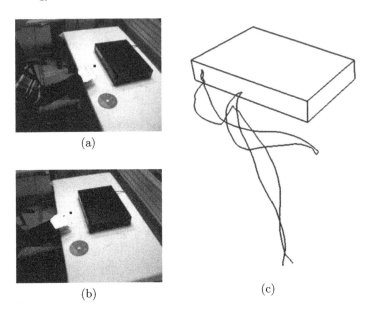

(a)

(b)

(c)

Fig. 1. (a), (b) a stereo pair from a 3D hand tracking experiment, (b) the computed hand trajectory in 3D

plot, the CD player has also been reconstructed in 3D. The 3D reconstruction of hand contours is achieved at 21 fps on a conventional Pentium IV processor.

2.3   Finger Detection

In many applications like the one dealt with in this paper, it is very important to be able to identify the fingertips of hands. Having already defined the contour of a hand, finger detection is performed by evaluating at several scales a curvature measure on contour points. The curvature measure assumes values in the range $[0.0, 1.0]$ and is defined as

$$K_l(P) = \frac{1}{2}\left[1 + \frac{\overrightarrow{P_1P} \cdot \overrightarrow{PP_2}}{||\overrightarrow{P_1P}|| \; ||\overrightarrow{PP_2}||} \right], \tag{1}$$

where P_1, P and P_2 are successive points on the contour, P being separated from P_1 and P_2 by the same number of contour points l. The symbol $(\cdot)$ denotes the vector dot product. The algorithm for finger detection computes $K_l(P)$ for all contour points of a hand and at various scales (i.e. for various values of the parameter l). A contour point P is then characterized as the location of a fingertip if both of the following conditions are met:

- $K_l(P)$ exceeds a certain threshold for at least one of the examined scales, and,
- $K_l(P)$ is a local maximum in its (scale-dependent) neighborhood of the contour.

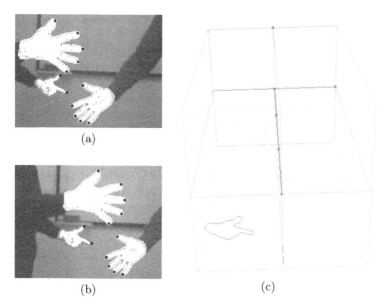

(a)

(b)   (c)

Fig. 2. (a), (b) a stereo pair from a 3D hand tracking experiment; hand contour points identified as fingers appear as black squares, (c) the estimated 3D hand contours. The origin of the coordinate system is at the far face of the parallelepiped.

Figures 2(a),(b) show the left and the right image from a sequence in a 3D hand tracking and finger detection experiment. In this experiment, there exist several hands which are successfully tracked among images. Fingers are also detected and denoted with the aid of black squares. Figure 2(c) shows the 3D reconstruction of the contours of the tracked hands which was achieved as described in section 2.2. In the reported experiments, the curvature threshold of the first criterion was set to 0.7.

3   From Gestures to Mouse Control

The 2D and 3D trackers that were previously described provide the perceptual input for defining a set of hand gestures through which gesture-based control of a computer's mouse can be exercised. We have defined two such gesture vocabularies, one based on the perceptual input supplied by 2D tracking and one based on that supplied by 3D tracking. In both cases, the set of gestures have been defined according to the following criteria:

- *Intuitiveness and ergonomics:* The defined gestures should be easy to learn and use.
- *Lack of ambiguity and ease of recognition:* The definition of the hand gestures should facilitate their automatic interpretation.

In the remainder of this section, we describe the two defined sets of gestures.

3.1 Mouse Control Based on 2D Hand Gestures

The defined 2D gesture vocabulary involves *static gestures*, i.e., gestures in which the information to be communicated lies in the hand and finger posture at a certain moment in time. To avoid errors due to image noise, it is assumed that these hand postures last for at least a short, fixed amount of time. In the actual implementation of the system, a minimum duration of half a second is employed. Assuming a frame rate of 30Hz, this means that in order to recognize a certain posture, this has to be maintained for a minimum of fifteen consecutive image frames.

The 2D hand gestures involve both hands of a user, each of which has a special role. More specifically, one hand is responsible for moving the mouse pointer and is therefore called the "pointer hand". The other hand is mainly responsible for issuing different commands and is therefore called the "commanding hand". These roles are not statically determined but can be chosen by the user: The first hand that appears in the field of view of the camera with one extended finger becomes the pointer hand. Then, the second appearing hand assumes the role of the commanding hand. Note that the roles of hands may be interchanged during system operation; This simply requires moving the hands out of the camera field of view and bringing them back in with the appropriate order and posture.

What follows, is a list of hand postures that the developed application is able to recognize, accompanied with their corresponding interpretation in the context of the computer mouse control application. Representative instances of these gestures can also be seen in Fig. 3.

- *Mouse control activation and deactivation:* In many cases, the user needs to activate and deactivate the interpretation of gesture-based commands for the mouse. This is achieved by a gesture involving both hands, each of which is presented with five extended fingers (see Fig. 3(a)). This posture toggles between the activation and the deactivation of gesture-based mouse control.
- *Mouse move:* This is achieved through the movement of the pointer hand (see Fig. 3(b)). The coordinates of the centroid of the pointer hand within the processed image are appropriately mapped to mouse cursor coordinates on the computer's desktop. The hand centroid is selected because its coordinates are less susceptible to image noise. Moreover, this makes the system's operation independent of the number of extended fingers. Nevertheless, the hand centroid cannot easily be located in extreme image positions (i.e. those close to its top, bottom, left and right borders). For this reason, strips along image borders are excluded from consideration; the rest of the image is then linearly mapped onto the computer's desktop.
- *Press left mouse button:* The commanding hand shows five extended fingers (see Fig. 3(c)).
- *Release left mouse button:* The commanding hand shows less than five extended fingers after a detected "press left mouse button" event.
- *Left mouse button click:* This is achieved by the combination of a "press left mouse button" and a "release left mouse button" gesture.

(a)   (b)   (c)   (d)   (e)

Fig. 3. Representative instances of the gestures used to control the mouse pointer (a) activate and deactivate gesture-based mouse control, (b) mouse move, (c) left button click, (d) right button click and, (e) left button double click

- *Right mouse button click:* The pointer hand presents five extended fingers (see Fig. 3(d)).
- *Left mouse button double click:* The commanding hand shows three extended fingers (see Fig. 3(e)).

At this point, it should be noted that in contrast to previous methods such as [14, 5], our approach does not require the presence in the image of any artificial objects for defining and/or supporting hand gestures. Based on the above set of gestures, the user of the system may also perform other useful mouse operations such as mouse drag-and-drop. This is naturally implemented as a "press left mouse button" gesture with the commanding hand, followed by a move operation achieved with the pointer hand and finally by a "release left mouse button" gesture, again by the commanding hand.

3.2   Mouse Control Based on 3D Hand Gestures

The key idea behind the definition of a vocabulary involving 3D gestures is that additional information can be conveyed to the system depending on the distance of the hand(s) from the camera system. Contrary to the case of the 2D vocabulary, the 3D one requires gestures of only one hand, with the exception of the case of activation and deactivation of the gesture-based mouse control. Another important difference is that the set of gestures includes two *dynamic gestures* as opposed to the strictly static ones employed in the 2D case. The complete 3D gestures vocabulary is as follows:

- *Mouse control activation and deactivation:* This is implemented as in the 2D vocabulary, i.e. ten extended fingers detected in both hands. As soon as mouse activation is detected, the distance between the commanding hand and the camera is estimated and considered as a reference distance for interpreting other gestures.
- *Choice of the pointer hand:* The pointer hand is the one that is closest to the camera.
- *Press left mouse button:* The pointer hand is extended towards the camera with none of its fingers extended. This is a dynamic gesture that is recognized based on posture characteristics (zero extended fingers) and the decrease of the distance of the pointer hand from the camera system.
- *Release left mouse button:* The pointer hand roughly retracts back to the reference distance after a "press left mouse button" gesture.

- *Left mouse button click:* Implemented as the combination of a "press left mouse button" gesture followed by a "release left mouse button".
- *Right mouse button click:* Similar to the left mouse button click, with the difference that the pointer hand has five extended fingers instead of none.
- *Left mouse button double click:* Similar to the left and right mouse button clicks, with the difference that the pointer hand has three extended fingers.

4   Experiments and Validation

The developed methods for controlling a computer mouse through 2D and 3D hand gestures have been extensively tested in several real world situations. The focus of the conducted experiments was not on the robustness and the performance of the supporting 2D and 3D hand tracker components since these have been extensively reported elsewhere [1, 2]. Instead, the focus was on assessing the usability and the ergonomics of each of the proposed human-computer interfaces and on comparing their relative performance.

As a first step, ten of our colleagues were introduced to the operation of both interfaces and were asked to perform certain mouse functions by employing both of them. One specific task that the users were asked to perform was to launch the MS Paint application, move the MS Paint window away from its popup location, select the free pencil tool, a specific pen size, a shape and a color and write a small piece of text on the image canvas. This type of test requires the use of all gestures. Analogous tests were designed involving the operation of the calculator application. Figure 4 shows an example of what one of the users scribbled by using the 2D gestures interface. The quality of the text shows that the developed interface supports smooth and accurate control of the mouse pointer and the button events triggered by hand gestures. This is particularly important, especially if one takes into account that a 200×280 window of the processed image was linearly mapped onto a 1024×768 computer desktop.

User experiences were then gathered and evaluated. The general conclusions drawn can be summarized as follows. The 3D gestures are more easy to understand and assimilate compared to the 2D gestures. An additional advantage of the 3D set is the fact that, excluding mouse activation and deactivation, only one hand is required to operate the mouse. The users also found very intuitive the implementation of the various mouse clicks as a hand motion towards the camera, followed by a hand motion towards the torso because this is analogous to pressing an imaginary 3D button.

However, the same users found the interface based on the 2D gestures more responsive and therefore much more user-friendly. This is attributed to the higher frame rate that is achievable in the single camera setting compared to the stereo one. An additional disadvantage of the 3D interface is the fact that mouse click, although more intuitive, is less accurate compared to its 2D counterpart. This is because the commanding hand and the pointer hand coincide. Therefore, if a user does not move his hand in a direction strictly perpendicular to the image plane, this affects the desktop location on which the image

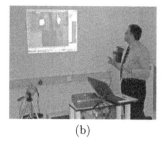

(a)   (b)

Fig. 4. (a) Text scribbled by a user operating the MS Paint application using the 2D gestures mouse control interface. (b) A snapshot from an experiment where the developed mouse control interface is being used to control a MS PowerPoint presentation. The employed system of cameras can be seen at the lower right corner of this image.

click is issued. As a general remark, the consensus among the users participating in these usability tests was that the set of 3D gestures is probably more appropriate for the novice user. However, after some user training and acquaintance with the gestures of the 2D interface, the former constitutes a much preferred choice. This conclusion has been also validated by tests involving experienced users of the system that were able to control and run formal MS PowerPoint presentations in real-world conditions for extended (i.e., more than half an hour) periods of time. A snapshot from such a presentation is shown in Fig. 4(b). A representative video from such an experiment can be found at http://www.ics.forth.gr/~argyros/research/virtualmouse.htm. The increased user acceptance of the 2D interface over the 3D one is also important from a technical point of view, since the former has less hardware requirements (one, as opposed to two cameras), less setup effort (no need for stereo calibration, better portability, etc) and lower computational requirements. Finally, it is also worth mentioning that the permissible volume for moving the hands is smaller in the case of the 3D interface. This is because it requires the hands to be visible in both cameras, thus restricting them to lie in a space smaller than the visual pyramid of any camera alone.

5   Summary

In this paper, we proposed two different systems for human-computer interaction based on hand gestures. More specifically, two different hand gesture vocabularies were proposed for remotely operating the mouse of a computer. One of the developed vocabularies is based on static, 2D hand postures while the second relies on 3D information and uses a mixture of static and dynamic gestures. Both interfaces have been extensively tested and their relative advantages and disadvantages have been assessed. Overall, both proposed approaches are robust and capable of supporting vision-based HCI in real-world situations. However, the 2D one seems preferable to the trained user.

From a design and implementation point of view, the proposed 2D and 3D hand gesture vocabularies and the computational techniques used to recognize them were kept quite simple. Clearly, much of the robustness of the proposed system is attributed to the quality and the stability of the underlying perceptual processes that transform raw image data into a symbolic description that is amenable to interpretation. Characteristics such as the accuracy of skin color detection under varying illumination conditions, the robustness of tracking several moving objects under severe occlusions and the capability of accurate segmentation of fingertips and extraction of 3D information are of paramount importance in terms of the usability of the developed system. Current efforts focus on the development of richer 2D and 3D sets of human-body gestures for increasing the information content in the interface between humans and computers.

Acknowledgements

This work has been partially supported by EU IST-2001-32184 project ActIPret and EU-IST NoE MUSCLE (FP6-507752). The contributions of Mickael Marechal, Benjamin Marie and Cedric Groyer in the implementation and testing of the proposed interface are gratefully acknowledged.

References

1. A.A. Argyros and M.I.A. Lourakis. Real Time Tracking of Multiple Skin-Colored Objects with a Possibly Moving Camera. In *Proceedings of ECCV'04*, pages 368–379, 2004.
2. A.A. Argyros and M.I.A. Lourakis. Binocular Hand Tracking and Reconstruction Based on 2D Shape Matching. *Submitted to ICPR'06, under review*, 2006.
3. P. Besl and N. McKay. A Method for Registration of 3-d Shapes. *IEEE Trans. on PAMI*, 14(2), 1992.
4. D. Chetverikov, D. Svirko, D. Stepanov, and P. Krsek. The Trimmed Iterative Closest Point Algorithm. In *Proceedings of ICPR'02*, 2002.
5. J.J. Corso, D. Burschka, and G.D. Hager. The 4D Touchpad: Unencumbered HCI With VICs. In *Proceedings of CVPR-HCI'03*, page 55, 2003.
6. D. Gale and L.S. Shapley. College Admissions and the Stability of Marriage. *American Mathematical Monthly*, 69(9), 1962.
7. R. Goldman. Intersection of two lines in three-space. *In Graphics Gems I*, page 304, 1990.
8. S. Malik and J. Laszlo. Visual Touchpad: A Two-Handed Gestural Input Device. In *Proceedings of ICMI'04*, pages 289–296, 2004.
9. M. Porta. Vision-based User Interfaces: Methods and Applications. *Int. J. Human-Computer Studies*, 57(1):27–73, 2002.
10. P. Robertson, R. Laddaga, and M. van Kleek. Virtual Mouse Vision Based Interface. In *Proceedings of IUI'04*, pages 177–183, 2004.
11. P. J. Rousseeuw. Least Median of Squares Regression. *Journal of American Statistics Association*, 79:871–880, 1984.

12. A. van Dam. Post-WIMP User Interfaces. *Commun. ACM*, 40(2):63–67, 1997.
13. Z. Zhang. Determining the Epipolar Geometry and its Uncertainty: a Review. *Int. Journal of Computer Vision*, 27:161–195, 1998.
14. Z. Zhang, Y. Wu, Y. Shan, and S. Shafer. Visual Panel: Virtual Mouse, Keyboard and 3D Controller With an Ordinary Piece of Paper. In *Proceedings of PUI'01*, pages 1–8, 2001.

Computing Emotion Awareness Through Facial Electromyography

Egon L. van den Broek[1,2], Marleen H. Schut[2,3], Joyce H.D.M. Westerink[4],
Jan van Herk[4], and Kees Tuinenbreijer[3]

[1] Center for Telematics and Information Technology (CTIT) / Institute for Behavioral Research
(IBR), University of Twente,
P.O. box 217, 7500 AE Enschede, The Netherlands
e.l.vandenbroek@utwente.nl
[2] Department of Artificial Intelligence / Nijmegen Institute for Cognition and Information
(NICI), Radboud University Nijmegen,
P.O. Box 9104, 6500 HE Nijmegen, The Netherlands
e.vandenbroek@nici.ru.nl, mhschut@student.ru.nl
[3] Philips Consumer Electronics, The Innovation Laboratories,
Glaslaan 2, SFJ 507 Eindhoven, The Netherlands
{marleen.schut, kees.tuinenbreijer}@philips.com
[4] Philips Research, High Tech Campus 34,
5656 AE Eindhoven, The Netherlands
{joyce.westerink, jan.van.herk}@philips.com

Abstract. To improve human-computer interaction (HCI), computers need to
recognize and respond properly to their user's emotional state. This is a fundamental application of affective computing, which relates to, arises from, or
deliberately influences emotion. As a first step to a system that recognizes emotions of individual users, this research focuses on how emotional experiences are
expressed in six parameters (i.e., mean, absolute deviation, standard deviation,
variance, skewness, and kurtosis) of physiological measurements of three electromyography signals: frontalis (EMG1), corrugator supercilii (EMG2), and zygomaticus major (EMG3). The 24 participants were asked to watch film scenes of
120 seconds, which they rated afterward. These ratings enabled us to distinguish
four categories of emotions: negative, positive, mixed, and neutral. The skewness
of the EMG2 and four parameters of EMG3, discriminate between the four emotion categories. This, despite the coarse time windows that were used. Moreover,
rapid processing of the signals proved to be possible. This enables tailored HCI
facilitated by an emotional awareness of systems.

1   Introduction

Computers are experienced by their users as coldhearted; i.e., "marked by lack of sym-
pathy, interest, or sensitivity" [1]. However, "during the past decade rapid advances
in spoken language technology, natural language processing, dialog modeling, multi-
modal interfaces, animated character design, and mobile applications all have stimu-
lated interest in a new class of conversational interfaces" [2]. The progress made in this
broad range of research and technology enables the rapid computation and modeling of

T.S. Huang et al. (Eds.): HCI/ECCV 2006, LNCS 3979, pp. 52–63, 2006.

empathy for human-computer interaction (HCI) purposes. The latter is of importance since conversation is, apart from being an information exchange, a social activity, which is inherently enforcing [2]. Futurists envision embodied, social artificial systems that interact in a natural manner with us. Such systems need to sense its user's emotional state and should be able to express emotions as well.

Empathic artificial systems can, for example, prevent user frustration in HCI. Users feel frequently frustrated by various causes; i.e., error messages, timed out / dropped / refused connections, freezes, long download time, and missing / hard-to-find features [3]. Picard [4] posed the prevention of user frustration as one of the main goals in HCI. When prevention is not sufficient, online reduction of frustration is needed. According to Hone, Akhtar, and Saffu [5], an (embodied) affective agent, using techniques of active listening and empathy could reduce user frustration.

The analysis of psychophysiological signals is also of use for the validation of computer vision systems that aim to recognize emotional expressions. Then, the latter systems' functioning can be validated and optimized. Knowledge gained from studies on the expression of emotions can also be used for embodied agents, which can, consequently, express emotions in a more realistic manner [6].

The current paper discusses the emotion and their expression through psychophysiological measures, in Section 2 and Section 3. Next, in Section 4, affective wearables are introduced in which the proposed apparatus for the measurement of the psychophysiological signals can be embedded. Next, the setup of the experiment that is conducted is described in Section 5, followed by a reduction of the data, in Section 6. The results are described in Section 7. The paper ends with Section 8 in which the results are discussed, limitations are denoted, and future research is described.

2 Emotion

Despite the complexity of the concept emotion, most researchers agree that emotions are acute, intentional states that exist in a relatively short period of time and are related to a particular event, object, or action [7, 8]. In relation with physiology, emotions are predominantly described as points in a two dimensional space of affective valence and arousal, in which valence represents overall pleasantness of emotional experiences ranging from negative to positive, while arousal represents the intensity level of emotion, ranging from calm to excited [9, 10].

The simplest differentiation of emotions is a differentiation between positive and negative emotions. In most cases of HCI, this is sufficient to improve the dialog between user and computer; e.g., when a user has a negative emotion, the computer can adapt its dialog to that, depending on the context. The valence-arousal model differentiates between emotions on both valence (positive and negative affect) and arousal (intensity of the emotion), which allows us to tell the difference between four rough categories of emotions, when differentiated between high valence and low valence and high arousal and low arousal. Some researchers even differentiated between nine categories by including a neutral section on both the valence and arousal axis. However, an, in principle, infinite amount of other arbitrary number of categories can be defined, where the valence and arousal axis not necessarily are divided with the same precision [11].

With the determination of emotions, using the valence-arousal model, two difficulties occur: the problem of the lack of extreme coordinates in two categories of the valence-arousal model and the category of emotions, which is called mixed emotions. The first difficulty is mentioned by Lang, Bradley, and Cuthbert [12]. They generated a database of affective pictures (the International Affective Picture System; IAPS). All IAPS pictures were judged according to the valence and arousal dimensions, which resulted in a boomerang shaped figure, with its two extremes in the quadrants high valence – high arousal, and low valence –high arousal. Despite their great efforts, Lang, Bradley, and Cuthbert [12] failed to find pictures that represent the extremities of all four categories.

The second difficulty, mixed emotions, occur when an event, object, or action triggers more than one emotion; e.g., a person feels happy because he sees his old aunt again after many years, but sad because his aunt does not seem to be very healthy anymore. The valence-arousal model, as a two-dimensional space, cannot handle this kind of data; however, the valence-arousal model might be capable of coping with mixed emotions; Konijn and Hoorn [13] suggest that in order to cope with mixed emotions, the valence axis should be unipolar instead of bipolar. They referred to earlier research, which showed that reverse affects do not necessarily have strong negative correlations. When valence is rated on two scales, one for the intensity of positive affect and one for the intensity of negative affect, mixed emotions, in the sense of both positive and negative emotions, will show. As an extension to the valence-arousal model, a unipolar valence axis, with separated positive and negative axes, might allow for a better discrimination between different emotions.

In the current research, solely the valence axis was explored. The reason for this, in addition to the afore mentioned problems of the valence-arousal model, is twofold: 1) As a first step to recognize emotions accurately in a long time window (120 sec.), it is necessary to start with simple categories, and 2) Valence has been proved to influence EMG [14].

3   Psychophysiological Measures

The research area that considers the effect of psychological processes on physiology is called psychophysiology. The roots of the first psychophysiological area emotions lay in Darwin's book "The expression of emotions in man and animals", which he wrote in 1872. From then on research in psychophysiology has known periods of extensive popularity and even so periods of unpopularity or even rejection. After a period of the latter category, psychophysiology gains interest again due to affective computing.

The overall assumption is that emotion arouses the autonomic nervous system (ANS), which alters the physiological state. This is expressed in various physiological measures; e.g., heart rate, blood pressure, respiration rate, galvanic skin response [15]. In addition, Alpha and Beta brain waves are used to access human attention and emotion [16]. The main advantage of using autonomic physiological measures is that autonomic variables are regulated by the ANS, which controls functions outside the individual's conscious control [15].

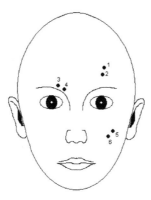

Fig. 1. The points the electrodes that were placed on the face of the participants to determine the EMG signals. The EMG signals of the frontalis, corrugator supercilii, and zygomaticus major were respectively measured through electrodes 1-2, 3-4, and 5-6.

In this research, we focused on how emotional experiences, rated to their positive and negative affect, are expressed in three electromyography (EMG) signals: frontalis, corrugator supercilii, and zygomaticus major (see also Figure 1). The choice of these measures is twofold: 1) a great deal of emotional expression is located in the face [14], as can be measured using facial EMG and 2) the EMG signals can be used to validate computer vision algorithms that aim to detect the emotional expression of people.

EMG measures muscle activity of a certain muscle. Facial EMG is related to affective valence; however, the type of relation depends strongly on the muscle that is measured. The corrugator supercilii, which causes a frown when activated, increases linearly with a decrease in valence, while the zygomaticus major, which is responsible for smiling when activated, increases with an increase in valence [12].

In the Section 5, we will describe the experiment in which the above introduced psychophysiological measures are used in order to verify whether or not they express the emotional state of humans. However, first we will introduce affective wearables in the next section. Such pervasive technology facilitates a system in monitoring its user in an unobtrusive manner. This enables the system to conduct affective computing, which will facilitate in efficient and as pleasant experienced HCI.

4   Affective Wearables

Direct physiological measures are often considered to be obtrusive to the user; this is not necessarily true. In the field of affective computing, some efforts have been made to design unobtrusive measurement technology: affective wearables. Picard and Healy [8], define an affective wearable as "a wearable system equipped with sensors and tools which enables recognition of its wearer's affective patterns".

Affective wearables become smaller in time, due to improved design and smaller technology components. Especially when hidden in daily used tools and objects, affective wearables could make a huge difference in user acceptance of direct physiological measures.

The acceptance of direct physiological measurements is of great importance since indirect physiological measurement are much more subject to noise. Indirect physiological measurements (e.g., through voice analysis [17]) have been applied in controlled settings such as telepsychiatry [18] and evaluation of therapy effectiveness [17]. However, outside such controlled conditions these measures have not proved to be reliable.

Measurement of physiological signals have already been embedded into wearable tools; e.g., Picard and Scheirer [19] designed the 'Galvactivator', a glove that detects the skin conductivity and maps its values into a led display. In an overview of previous work of the Affective Computing Research Group at MIT, Picard [20] describes several affective wearables. One affective wearable that is of interest in this research is the expression glasses. The expression glasses sense facial movements, which are recognized as affective patterns.

5   Method

5.1   Subjects

24 Subjects (20 female) were invited from a volunteers database. They signed an informed consent form, and were awarded with a small incentive for their participation. They were aged between 27 and 59 years (average 43 years).

5.2   Materials

Sixteen film sequences were selected for their emotional content. Several of these sequences were described by Gross and Levenson [21] for their capability of eliciting one unique emotion among various viewers. They were edited with Dutch subtitles, as is normal on Dutch TV and in Dutch cinemas. Since not enough material of Gross and Levenson [21] was available with Dutch subtitles in acceptable quality, the set was completed with a number of similar sequences. The resulting video fragments each lasted between 9 seconds and 4 minutes. If the fragment lasted less than 120 sec., a plain blue screen was added to make a total of 120 sec.

The film fragments were presented on a large 42" 16 : 9 flat panel screen mounted on the wall of the room. Print-outs for significant scenes of each of the film fragments were used to jog the subjects memory of each film fragment after the viewing session.

The psychophysiological measurements were performed with a TMS Portilab system connected to a computer. A ground electrode was attached to the right-hand lower chest area.

Three EMG measurements were done: at the left-hand corrugator supercilii muscle, the right-hand zygomaticus major muscle and the frontalis muscle above the left eye. At each site 2 electrodes were placed in the direction of the muscle (see Figure 1). These signals were first high pass filtered at 20Hz and then the absolute difference of the two electrodes was average filtered with a time constant of 0.2 sec.

5.3 Procedure

At the beginning of the session, the subject was invited to take place in a comfortable chair and the electrodes were positioned: first at the chest, then at the fingers and then at the face. Then, the recording equipment was checked and aligned when needed. A rest period of 5 minutes was taken into account The subjects were presented with the 16 video fragments, each segment was presented only once.

A pseudo-random order of presentation was generated for the 16 video presentations. This order was designed to spread positive and negative scenes evenly over the session. It was presented to 12 subjects, each starting with a different scene in the list, but maintaining the same order. The reverse order was presented to the other 12 subjects, again each starting with a different scene while maintaining the same presentation order. In between two fragments a plain blue screen was presented for 120 seconds.

After the measuring session, the electrodes were detached, and the subject was requested to fill out a short questionnaire. In this questionnaire, representative pictures of the 16 video fragments were represented sequentially, and the subject was requested to rate them according to various emotion-related axes; e.g., intensity of positive feelings when watching the fragment, and the same for negative feelings.

6   Data Reduction

Average intensities for both positive and negative ratings were calculated for each of the film fragments, allowing for a classification of the fragments in 4 emotion categories:

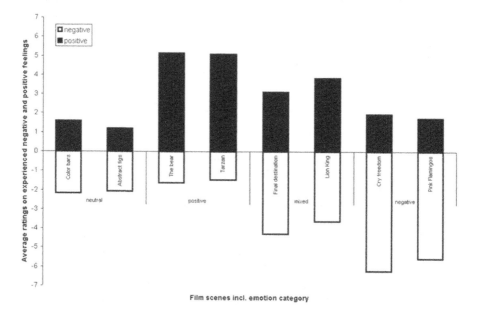

Fig. 2. The eight film scenes with the average ratings given by subjects on both experienced negative and positive feelings. These ratings categorized the film scened into four emotion categories: neutral, mixed, positive, and negative.

neutral, mixed, positive, negative. In each emotion category, the two fragments with a duration closest to 120 seconds were selected for further analysis (see Figure 2 and Table 1). Furthermore, the EMG data of two subjects appeared to be corrupt; therefore, these datasets were not analyzed.

The three EMG (of the frontalis, corrugator supercilii, and zygomaticus major) signals were measured in order to determine their discriminating ability on the four emotion categories induced by the eight films. To determine the latter, six parameters (mean, absolute deviation, standard deviation, variance, skewness, and kurtosis) were derived from the four signals.

Where the mean, standard deviation, and average deviation are well-known dimensional quantities (i.e., have the same units as the measured quantities x_j), the skewness and kurtosis are conventionally defined as non-dimensional quantities. Both skewness and kurtosis are less well known statistical measures and both are defined in several ways [22, 23]. Therefore, we provide the definitions as adopted in the current research.

The skewness characterizes the degree of asymmetry of a distribution around its mean. It characterizes the shape of the distribution. The usual definition is [22, 23, 24]:

$$\text{Skewness}(x_1 \ldots x_N) = \frac{1}{N} \sum_{j=1}^{N} \left[\frac{x_j - \overline{x}}{\sigma} \right]^3 \tag{1}$$

where $\sigma = \sigma(x_1 \ldots x_N)$ is the distribution's standard deviation. A positive value of skewness signifies a distribution with an asymmetric tail extending out towards more positive x; a negative value signifies a distribution whose tail extends out towards more negative x.

Kurtosis measures the relative peakedness or flatness of a distribution relative to a normal distribution. We applied kurtosis as [22, 23, 24]:

$$\text{Kurtosis}(x_1 \ldots x_N) = \left\{ \frac{1}{N} \sum_{j=1}^{N} \left[\frac{x_j - \overline{x}}{\sigma} \right]^4 \right\} - 3 \tag{2}$$

where the -3 term makes the value zero for a normal distribution.

The skewness and kurtosis of EMG signals have been topic of research in previous studies. However, the use of skewness and kurtosis as discriminating descriptors is very limited to only a few studies. In 1983, Cacioppo, Marshall-Goodell, and Dorfman [25] analyzed among a number of parameters, the skewness and kurtosis of skeletal muscle patterns, recorded through EMGs. Four years later, a paper of Cacioppo and Dorfman [24] is published that discusses "waveform moment analysis in psychophysiological research" in general.

In 1989, Hess et al. [26] conducted research toward experiencing and showing happy feelings, also using video segments. Hess et al. [26] recorded four facial EMG signals and extracted the mean, variance, skewness, and kurtosis of these signals. The current

Table 1. The eight film scenes with the average ratings given by subjects on both experienced negative and positive feelings. Based on the latter two dimensions, the four emotion categories: neutral, mixed, positive, and negative are founded.

Film scene	Positive	Negative	Emotion category
Color bars	1.60	2.20	neutral
Abstract figures	1.20	2.10	
The bear	5.15	1.65	positive
Tarzan	5.10	1.50	
Final destination	3.11	4.32	mixed
Lion King	3.85	3.65	
Cry freedom	1.95	6.25	negative
Pink flamingos	1.75	5.60	
Average	2.96	3.41	

research is distinct from that of Hess et al. [26] since it distinguishes four emotion categories instead of the presence or absence of only one.

7   Results

For each of the six statistical parameters, the complete EMG signals were processed over 120 seconds, which was the duration of the films; see also the previous section. For each parameter of each physiological measure, a repeated measures ANOVA was conducted, with the four emotions, each measured with two film scenes, as within-subject factors. So, a total of $18 (3 \times 6)$ repeated measures ANOVAs were conducted.

The EMG of the frontalis muscle (see Figure 1) did not provide a significant discrimination between the four emotion categories on any of the statistical parameters. Of all physiological measures, the zygomaticus major signal is the most discriminative physiological signal. The mean, absolute deviation, standard deviation and variance calculated over the zygomaticus major EMG signal showed strong significant effects of emotions, as is illustrated in Figure 3. A significant effect did also show in the skewness of the corrugator supercilii EMG signal (see Figure 3). This is in line with results of previous research of Larsen, Norris, and Cacioppo [14], who concluded that valence influences both the corrugator supercilii and the zygomaticus major.

Not all investigated parameters of all EMG signals proved to be equally suited for sensing a human's emotional state. In particular, the 120 sec. averaged values of the physiological signals did not yield significant effects of emotion category, in contrast to what is generally reported in literature. One of the reasons might be that we chose not to correct our data for baseline values, as is common in psychophysiological literature. Another factor is that the present analysis was chosen to extend over a relatively long period of time including the beginning of the video fragment in which the targeted emotions were still in the process of getting elicited, which might have diminished the differences between categories of emotions. Nevertheless, even under these demanding analysis conditions, still some of the measures succeed in distinguishing between the respective emotion categories, as is shown in Figure 3.

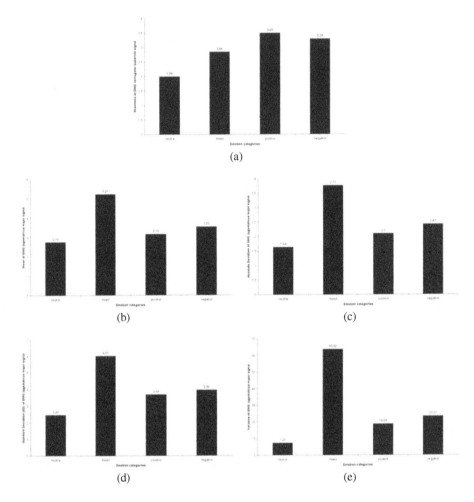

Fig. 3. The discriminating parameters per emotion category: a) Skewness of EMG corrugator supercilii signal (F(3,18) = 3.500, p<0.037) and of the EMG zygomaticus major signal the: b) mean (F(3,18) = 9.711, p<0.001), c) absolute deviation (F(3,18) = 8.369, p<0.001), d) standard deviation (SD) (F(3,18) = 5.837, p<0.006), and e) Variance (F(3,18) = 4.064, p<0.023).

8 Discussion

Designers envision electronic environments that are sensitive and responsive to the presence and emotion of people. This vision is baptized: "ambient intelligence" and is characterized as embedded, aware, natural, personalized, adaptive, and anticipatory. The set of psychophysiological measures as introduced suits this vision since it can be embedded in wearables, it facilitates awareness for systems connected to it, it aims to mimic human empathy (i.e., is natural), can be connected to a user-profile, senses user's changing emotions, and can facilitate in utilizing knowledge to anticipate on people's emotion and adapt its communication strategy.

For all four physiological signals used, the parameter skewness proved to be an interesting source of information. The skewness of the distributions of the data of two of the physiological signals differs significantly and for the remaining signal a trend is present, over the four emotions. The skewness characterizes the degree of asymmetry of a distribution around its mean. To inspect the distributions of the signals, more detailed analyzes have to be conducted. Measures such as the peak density should be taken into account for further analysis.

In addition to adding more descriptors of the physiological signals, the time windows of measurement can be changed. In the current setup, the time window enclosed the complete length of the film scene. However, smaller time windows (e.g., 10 or 30 sec.) can be applied. Moreover, dynamic time windows can be applied that enclose the time direct after a critical event (if any) appeared in the film scene. The drawback of the latter approach is that it can not be applied in practice, where it can be expected to prove good results for data gathered through experimentation, as in the current research.

A noteworthy observation in the results is that activation of the zygomaticus major EMG shows lower values of the mean, absolute deviation, standard deviation and variance in response to the neutral stimuli than on the other stimuli (see Figure 3). However, a pure neutral stimulus should, in contrast to stimuli of the other emotion categories, not excite a participant at all. In particular in the variance of the zygomaticus major, the difference between neutral emotions and other emotions is shown. This could imply that these statistic values are not only influenced by valence, but by arousal too. Future research should address this issue.

Larsen, Norris and Cacioppo [14] concluded that valence had a stronger effect on the corrugator supercilii than on the zygomaticus major in experiencing standardized affective pictures, sounds, and words, while our research shows a stronger effect of emotions on the zygomaticus major, than on the corrugator supercilii. In addition, the effect is present with four statistical parameters of the zygomaticus major, where it is only present in one statistical parameter (skewness) of the corrugator supercilii.

The difference in strength of the effects found between the current research and that of Larsen, Norris, and Cacioppo [14] can be explained by the fact that other statistical parameters were used in the current research than in that of Larsen, Norris, and Cacioppo [14]. Another difference between the two researches is the type of stimuli. Film scenes are dynamic and multi-modal, they induce emotions by both auditory, and dynamic visual stimuli, as well as affective words, in some fragments. The dynamic and multi-modal characteristics of the film scenes also provide good means to build up emotions, or to create a shock effect. This is not possible with affective words, sounds or pictures of a static character as often used in research to the axes of the valence-arousal model. On the one hand, all these factors give film scenes a relatively high degree of ecological validity [21]. On the other hand, it can not be determined which modality influences the emotional state of the subjects to the highest extent.

A more general notion that can have a significant impact on measurement of emotions is that the emotional state of people changes over time, due to various circumstances. Moreover, different persons have different emotional experiences over the same events, objects, or actions. The latter is determined by a person's personality. Personality traits correlate with affective states, especially with the personality traits extraversion and neuroticism, which have been linked both theoretically and empirically to the fundamental affective states of positive and negative affect, respectively [27]. Hence, to enable tailored communication strategies in HCI, not only the emotional state of a person should be determined but also his personality. Providing that the system possesses a personality profile of its user, it will be able to react appropriately to its user's emotions by selecting a suitable communication strategy.

A set of psychophysiological signals is discussed that mirrors one's psychological state up to a high extent; hence, it provides the means to unravel the intriguing feature of humans to sense the emotions of other humans. With that, a first step is made toward a new generation of computer systems. In time, these systems will be able to communicate and debate with us and penetrate our emotional state. Then, computer systems would truly be evolved from coldhearted to warmhearted systems.

References

1. Merriam-Webster, Incorporated: Merriam-Webster Online. URL: http://www.m-w.com/ ([Last accessed on February 6, 2006])
2. Oviatt, S.L., Darves, C., Coulston, R.: Toward adaptive conversational interfaces: Modeling speech convergence with animated personas. ACM Transactions on Computer-Human Interaction **11** (2004) 300–328
3. Ceaparu, I., Lazar, J., Bessiere, K., Robinson, J., Shneiderman, B.: Determining causes and severity of end-user frustration. International Journal of Human-Computer Interaction **17** (2004) 333–356
4. Picard, R.: Affective computing for HCI. In: Proceedings of HCI International (the 8th International Conference on Human-Computer Interaction) on Human-Computer Interaction: Ergonomics and User Interfaces. Volume 1., Lawrence Erlbaum Associates, Inc.: Mahwah, NJ, USA (1999) 829–833
5. Hone, K., Akhtar, F., Saffu, M.: Affective agents to reduce user frustration: the role of agent embodiment. In: Proceedings of Human-Computer Interaction (HCI2003), Bath, UK (2003)
6. Albrecht, I., Schröder, M., Haber, J., Seidel, H.: Mixed feelings: expression of non-basic emotions in a muscle-based talking head. Virtual Reality **8** (2005) 201–212
7. Ortony, A., Clore, G.L., Collins, A.: The cognitive structure of emotions. Cambridge, New York: Cambridge University Press (1988)
8. Picard, R.: Affective Computing. Boston MA.: MIT Press (1997)
9. Ball, G., Breese, J.: Modeling the emotional state of computer users. In: Workshop on Attitude, Personality and Emotions in User-Adapted Interaction, Banff, Canada (1999)
10. Lang, P.J.: The emotion probe: Studies of motivation and attention. American Psychologist **52** (1995) 372–385
11. Bosma, W., André, E.: Exploiting emotions to disambiguate dialogue acts. In: Proceedings of the 9th International Conference on Intelligent User Interface, Funchal, Madeira, Portugal, ACM Press: New York, NY, USA (2004) 85–92
12. Lang, P.J., Bradley, M.M., Cuthbert, B.N.: motion, motivation, and anxiety: Brain mechanisms and psychophysiology. Biological Psychiatry **44** (1998) 1248–1263
13. Konijn, E.A., Hoorn, J.F.: Some like it bad. Testing a model for perceiving and experiencing fictional characters. Media Psychology **7** (2005) 107–144
14. Larsen, J.T., Norris, C.J., Cacioppo, J.T.: Effects of positive and negative affect on electromyographic activity over zygomaticus major and corrugator supercilii. Psychophysiology **40** (2003) 776–785

15. Scerbo, M.W., Freeman, F.G., Mikulka, P.J., Parasuraman, R., Di Nocero, F.: The efficacy of psychophysiological measures for implementing adaptive technology. Technical Report NASA / TP-2001-211018, NASA Center for AeroSpace Information (CASI) (2001)
16. Aizawa, K., Ishijima, K., Shiina, M.: Summarizing wearable video. In: IEEE International Conference on Image Processing (ICIP). Volume 3., Thessaloniki, Greece (2001) 398–401
17. Van den Broek, E.L.: Emotional Prosody Measurement (EPM): A voice-based evaluation method for psychological therapy effectiveness. Studies in Health Technology and Informatics (Medical and Care Compunetics 1) **103** (2004) 118–125
18. Hilty, D.M., Marks, S.L., Urness, D., Yellowlees, P.M., Nesbitt, T.S.: Clinical and educational telepsychiatry applications: A review. The Canadian Journal of Psychiatry **49** (2004) 12–23
19. Picard., R.W., Scheirer, J.: The galvactivator: A glove that senses and communicates skin conductivity. In: Proceedings of the 9th International Conference on Human-Computer Interaction, New Orleans (2001)
20. Picard, R.W.: Toward computers that recognize and respond to user emotion. IBM Systems Journal **39** (2000) 705–719
21. Gross, J.J., Levenson, R.W.: Emotion elicitation using films. Cognition and Emotion **9** (1995) 87–108
22. Press, W.H., Flannery, B.P., Teukolsky, S.A., Vetterling, W.T.: Numerical recipes in C: The art of scientific computing. 2nd edn. Cambridge, England: Cambridge University Press (1992)
23. Weisstein, E.W.: CRC Concise Encyclopedia of Mathematics. 2nd edn. Chapman & Hall/CRC: USA (2002)
24. Cacioppo, J.T., Dorfman, D.D.: Waveform movement analysis in psychophysiological research. Psychological Bulletin **102** (1987) 421–438
25. Cacioppo, J.T., Marshall-Goodell, B., Dorfman, D.D.: Skeletal muscular patterning: Topographical analysis of the integrated electromyogram. Psychophysiology **20** (1983) 269–283
26. Hess, U., Kappas, A., McHugo, G.J., Kleck, R.E., Lanzetta, J.T.: An analysis of the encoding and decoding of spontaneous and posed smiles: The use of facial electromyography. Journal of Nonverbal Behavior **13** (1989) 121–137
27. Matzler, K., Faullant, R., Renzl, B., Leiter, V.: The relationship between personality traits (extraversion and neuroticism), emotions and customer self-satisfaction. Innovative Marketing **1** (2005) 32–39

Silhouette-Based Method for Object Classification and Human Action Recognition in Video

Yiğithan Dedeoğlu[1], B. Uğur Töreyin[2], Uğur Güdükbay[1], and A. Enis Çetin[2]

[1] Bilkent University, Department of Computer Engineering
{yigithan, gudukbay}@cs.bilkent.edu.tr
[2] Department of Electrical and Electronics Engineering,
06800, Bilkent, Ankara, Turkey
{bugur, cetin}@bilkent.edu.tr

Abstract. In this paper we present an instance based machine learning algorithm and system for real-time object classification and human action recognition which can help to build intelligent surveillance systems. The proposed method makes use of object silhouettes to classify objects and actions of humans present in a scene monitored by a stationary camera. An adaptive background subtracttion model is used for object segmentation. Template matching based supervised learning method is adopted to classify objects into classes like human, human group and vehicle; and human actions into predefined classes like walking, boxing and kicking by making use of object silhouettes.

1 Introduction

Classifying types and understanding activities of moving objects in video is both a challenging problem and an interesting research area with many promising applications. Our motivation in studying this problem is to design a human action recognition system that can be integrated into an ordinary visual surveillance system with real-time moving object detection, classification and activity analysis capabilities. The system is therefore supposed to work in real time. Considering the complexity of temporal video data, efficient methods must be adopted to create a fast, reliable and robust system. In this paper, we present such a system which operates on gray scale video imagery from a stationary camera.

In the proposed system moving object detection is handled by the use of an adaptive background subtraction scheme which reliably works both in indoor and outdoor environments [7].

After segmenting moving pixels from the static background of the scene, connected regions are classified into predetermined object categories: human, human group and vehicle. The classification algorithm depends on the comparison of the silhouettes of the detected objects with pre-labeled (classified) templates in an object silhouette database. The template database is created by collecting sample object silhouettes from sample videos and labeling them manually with appropriate categories. The silhouettes of the objects are extracted from the connected foreground regions by using a contour tracing algorithm [11].

T.S. Huang et al. (Eds.): HCI/ECCV 2006, LNCS 3979, pp. 64–77, 2006.

The action recognition system also exploits objects' silhouettes obtained from video sequences to classify actions. It mainly consists of two major steps: manual creation of silhouette and action templates offline and automatic recognition of actions in real-time. In classifying actions of humans into predetermined classes like walking, boxing and kicking; temporal signatures of different actions in terms of silhouette poses are used.

The remainder of this paper is organized as follows. Section 2 gives an overview of the related work. In the next two sections we give the details of moving object segmentation and object classification. In the next section, visual action recognition system is explained. Experimental results are discussed in Section 6 and finally we conclude the paper with Section 7.

2 Related Work

There have been a number of surveys about object detection, classification and human activity analysis in the literature [1, 9, 26].

Detecting regions corresponding to moving objects such as people and vehicles in video is the first basic step of almost every vision system because it provides a focus of attention and simplifies the processing on subsequent analysis steps. Due to dynamic changes in natural scenes such as sudden illumination and weather changes, repetitive motions that cause clutter (tree leaves moving in blowing wind), motion detection is a difficult problem to process reliably. Frequently used techniques for moving object detection are background subtraction, statistical methods, temporal differencing and optical flow [10, 12, 17, 22, 23, 26].

Moving regions detected in video may correspond to different objects in real-world such as pedestrians, vehicles, clutter, etc. It is very important to recognize the type of a detected object in order to track it reliably and analyze its activities correctly. Currently, there are two major approaches towards moving object classification which are shape-based and motion-based methods [26]. Shape-based methods make use of the objects' 2D spatial information like bounding rectangle, area, silhouette and gradient of detected object regions; whereas motion-based methods use temporally tracked features of objects for the classification solution.

The approach presented in [15] makes use of the objects' silhouette contour length and area information to classify detected objects into three groups: human, vehicle and other. The method depends on the assumption that humans are, in general, smaller than vehicles and have complex shapes. Dispersedness is used as the classification metric and it is defined as the square of contour length (perimeter) over object's are. Classification is performed at each frame and tracking results are used to improve temporal classification consistency.

The classification method developed by Collins et al. [7] uses view dependent visual features of detected objects to train a neural network classifier to recognize four classes: human, human group, vehicle and clutter. The inputs to the neural network are the dispersedness, area and aspect ratio of the object region and the camera zoom magnification. Like the previous method, classification is performed at each frame and results are kept in a histogram to improve temporal consistency of classification.

Some of the methods in the literature use only temporal motion features of objects in order to recognize their classes [6, 14, 27]. In general, they are used to distinguish non-rigid objects (e.g. human) from rigid objects (e.g. vehicles). The method proposed in [6] is based on the temporal self-similarity of a moving object. As an object that exhibits periodic motion evolves, its self-similarity measure also shows a periodic motion. The method exploits this clue to categorize moving objects using periodicity.

The systems for action recognition using video can be divided into three groups according to the methods they use: general signal processing techniques to match action signals, template matching and state-space approaches.

The first group treats the action recognition problem as a classification problem of the temporal activity signals of the objects according to pre-labeled reference signals representing typical human actions [26]. For instance Kanade et al. makes use of the signals generated by the change of the angle between the torso and the vertical line that passes through a human's body to distinguish walking and running patterns [7]. In another work Schuldt et al. make use of a local SVM approach to define local properties of complex motion patterns and classify the patterns using well known popular classifier Support Vector Machine [21]. General methods such as Dynamic time warping, Hidden Markov models and Neural Networks are used to process the action signals.

Second group of approaches converts image sequences into static shape patterns and in the recognition phase compares the patterns with pre-stored ones. For instance by using PCA, Chomat et al. created motion templates and a Bayes classifier was used to perform action recognition [4].

The last group considers each pose of the human body as a state and calculates a probability density function for each different action sequences [24]. A sequence can be thought of as a tour between different states. Hence the probability density function can be calculated from different tours of the same action. The probability functions than can be used to recognize test sequences.

3   Learning Scene Background for Segmentation

We use a combination of a background model and low-level image post-processing methods to create a foreground pixel map and extract object features at every video frame. Our implementation of background subtraction algorithm is partially inspired by the study presented in [7] and works on grayscale video imagery from a static camera. Background subtraction method initializes a reference background with the first few frames of video input. Then it subtracts the intensity value of each pixel in the current image from the corresponding value in the reference background image. The difference is filtered with an adaptive threshold per pixel to account for frequently changing noisy pixels. The reference background image and the threshold values are updated with an IIR filter to adapt to dynamic scene changes.

Let $I_n(x)$ represent the gray-level intensity value at pixel position (x) and at time instance n of video image sequence I which is in the range [0, 255]. Let $B_n(x)$ be the corresponding background intensity value for pixel position (x) estimated over time from video images I_0 through $I_n\text{-}1$. As the generic background subtraction scheme suggests, a pixel at position (x) in the current video image belongs to foreground if it satisfies:

$$|I_n(x) - B_n(x)| > T_n(x)$$

where $T_n(x)$ is an adaptive threshold value estimated using the image sequence I_0 through I_{n-1}. The above equation is used to generate the foreground pixel map which represents the foreground regions as a binary array where a 1 corresponds to a foreground pixel and a 0 stands for a background pixel. The reference background $B_n(x)$ is initialized with the first video image I_0, $B_0 = I_0$, and the threshold image is initialized with some pre-determined value (e.g. 15).

Since this system will be used in outdoor environments as well as indoor environments, the background model needs to adapt itself to the dynamic changes such as global illumination change (day night transition) and long term background update (parking a car in front of a building). Therefore the reference background and threshold images are dynamically updated with incoming images. The update scheme is different for pixel positions which are detected as belonging to foreground ($x \in FG$) and which are detected as part of the background ($x \in BG$):

$$B_{n+1}(x) = \begin{cases} \alpha B_n(x) + (1-\alpha)I_n(x), & x \in BG \\ \beta B_n(x) + (1-\beta)I_n(x), & x \in FG \end{cases}$$

$$T_{n+1}(x) = \begin{cases} \alpha T_n(x) + (1-\alpha)(\gamma \times |I_n(x) - B_n(x)|), & x \in BG \\ T_n(x), & x \in FG \end{cases}$$

where α, β and γ ($\in [0.0, 1.0]$) are learning constants which specify how much information from the incoming image is put to the background and threshold images.

The output of foreground region detection algorithm generally contains noise and therefore is not appropriate for further processing without special post-processing. Morphological operations, erosion and dilation [11], are applied to the foreground pixel map in order to remove noise that is caused by the first three of the items listed above. Our aim in applying these operations is to remove noisy foreground pixels that do not correspond to actual foreground regions and to remove the noisy background pixels near and inside object regions that are actually foreground pixels.

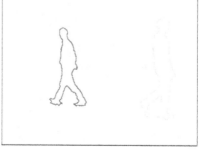

Fig. 1. Sample objects and their silhouettes

3.1 Calculating Object Features

After detecting foreground regions and applying post-processing operations to remove noise and shadow regions, the filtered foreground pixels are grouped into connected regions (blobs) and labeled by using a two-level connected component labeling algorithm presented in [11]. After finding individual blobs that correspond to objects, spatial features like bounding box, size, center of mass and silhouettes of these regions are calculated.

In order to calculate the center of mass point, $C_m = (x_{Cm}, y_{Cm})$, of an object O, we use the following equation [18]:

$$x_{C_m} = \frac{\sum_i^n x_i}{n}, \quad y_{C_m} = \frac{\sum_i^n y_i}{n}$$

where n is the number of pixels in O.

Both in offline and online steps of the classification algorithm, the silhouettes of the detected object regions are extracted from the foreground pixel map by using a contour tracing algorithm presented in [11]. Figure 1 shows sample detected foreground object regions and the extracted silhouettes. Another feature extracted from the object is the silhouette distance signal. Let $S = \{p_1, p_2,... , p_n\}$ be the silhouette of an object O consisting of n points ordered from top center point of the detected region in clockwise direction and C_m be the center of mass point of O. The distance signal $DS = \{d_1, d_2,... , d_n\}$ is generated by calculating the distance between C_m and each p_i starting from 1 through n as follows:

$$d_i = Dist(C_m, p_i), \quad \forall\, i \in [1 \ldots n]$$

where the *Dist* function is the Euclidian distance.

Different objects have different shapes in video and therefore have silhouettes of varying sizes. Even the same object has altering contour size from frame to frame. In order to compare signals corresponding to different sized objects accurately and to make the comparison metric scale-invariant we fix the size of the distance signal. Let N be the size of a distance signal DS and let C be the constant for fixed signal length. The fix-sized distance signal $\widehat{DS}$ is then calculated by sub-sampling or super-sampling the original signal DS as follows:

$$\widehat{DS}[i] = DS[i * \frac{N}{C}], \quad \forall\, i \in [1 \ldots C]$$

In the next step, the scaled distance signal $\widehat{DS}$ is normalized to have integral unit area. The normalized distance signal $\overline{DS}$ is calculated using the following equation:

$$\overline{DS}[i] = \frac{\widehat{DS}[i]}{\sum_1^n \widehat{DS}[i]}$$

Figure 2 shows a sample silhouette and its original and scaled distance signals.

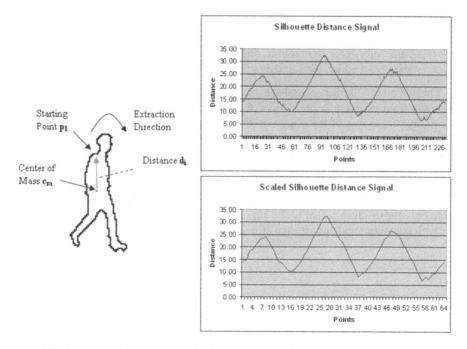

Fig. 2. Sample distance signal calculation and normal and scaled distance signals

4   Classifying Objects

The ultimate aim of different smart visual surveillance applications is to extract semantics from video to be used in higher level activity analysis tasks. Categorizing the type of a detected video object is a crucial step in achieving this goal. With the help of object type information, more specific and accurate methods can be developed to recognize higher level actions of video objects. Hence, we present a video object classification method based on object shape similarity to be used as a part of a "smart" visual surveillance system.

Typical video scenes may contain a variety of objects such as people, vehicles, animals, natural phenomenon (e.g. rain, snow), plants and clutter. However, main target of interest in surveillance applications are generally humans and vehicles.

The classification metric used in our method measures object similarity based on the comparison of silhouettes of the detected object regions extracted from the foreground pixel map with pre-labeled (manually classified) template object silhouettes stored in a database. The whole process of object classification method consists of two steps:

- Offline step: A template database of sample object silhouettes is created by manually labeling object types.
- Online step: The silhouette of each detected object in each frame is extracted and its type is recognized by comparing its silhouette based feature with the

ones in the template database in real time during surveillance. After the comparison of the object with the ones in the database, a template shape with minimum distance is found. The type of this object is assigned to the type of the object which we wanted to classify.

The template silhouette database is created offline by extracting several object contours from different scenes. Since the classification scheme makes use of object similarity, the shapes of the objects in the database should be representative poses of different object types. Figure 3 shows the template database we use for object classification. It consists of 24 different poses: 14 for human, 5 for human group and 5 for vehicles.

In classification step, our method does not use silhouettes in raw format, but rather compares converted silhouette distance signals. Hence, in the template database we store only the distance signal of the silhouette and the corresponding type information for both computational and storage efficiency.

Fig. 3. Sample object silhouette template database

4.1 Classification Metric

Our object classification metric is based on the similarity of object shapes. There are numerous methods in the literature for comparing shapes [20, 5, 18, 2, 13]. The reader is especially referred to the surveys presented in [25, 16] for good discussions on different techniques.

Our classification metric compares the similarity between the shapes of two objects, A and B, by finding the distance between their corresponding distance signals, DS_A and DS_B. The distance between two scaled and normalized distance signals, DS_A and DS_B is calculated as follows:

$$Dist_{AB} = \sum_{i=1}^{n} \left| \overline{DS}_A[i] - \overline{DS}_B[i] \right|$$

In order to find the type T_O of an object O, we compare its distance signal DS_O with all of the objects' distance signals in the template database. The type T_P of the template object P is assigned as the type of the query object O, $T_O = T_P$ where P satisfies the following:

$$Dist_{OP} \leq Dist_{OI}, \quad \forall \text{ object } I \text{ in the template database}$$

Figure 4 shows the silhouettes, silhouette signals and signal distances of a sample query object and template database objects for type classification.

Distance between two objects can be computed using more sophisticated methods such as dynamic programming providing a nonlinear warping of the horizontal axis [3] instead of the linear warping used in the calculation $Dist_{AB}$. However, a straightforward implementation of dynamic programming increases computational complexity and may not be suitable for the purposes of a real-time system.

In order to reduce noise in object classification a maximum likelihood scheme is adopted. The assigned object types are counted for a window of k ($= 5$) frames and the maximum one is assigned as the type. This reduces false classifications due to errors in segmentation.

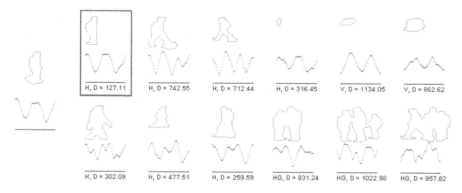

Fig. 4. Sample query object and its distances (D) to several objects in the silhouette template database. Object types are Human (H), Human Group (HG) and Vehicle (V). The matching object is shown with the bounding rectangle.

5   Recognizing Human Actions

After detecting the type of an object, if it is a human, its actions can be recognized. The action recognition system can recognize six different human actions which are: walking, boxing and kicking. Figure 6 shows video frames from sample sequences for these action types. The whole process of human action recognition method consists of two steps:

- Offline step: A pose template database by using human silhouettes for different poses is created. The silhouettes in this database are used to create a pose histogram which is used as an action template. An action template database is created by using these histograms calculated from sample action sequences.

- Online step: The silhouette of each detected human in each frame is extracted and its pose is matched with one in the pose template database. Then a histogram of the matched poses is created at each frame by using a history window of the matched human poses. Then the calculated histogram is matched against the ones in the template action database, and the label of the action with minimum distance is assigned as the current action label.

5.1 Creating Silhouette-Based Pose Template Database

A typical human action such as walking involves repetitive motion. Although throughout a video sequence several hundreds of silhouettes can be extracted for a subject, the shapes of the silhouettes will exhibit an almost periodic similarity. Hence, the basic set of shapes for a full period can represent an action. Furthermore, the key poses in the basic motion set show differences from action to action. For instance, the silhouettes of a walking person from side view can be represented with three key poses corresponding to the cases of full stretched legs, closed legs and partially stretched legs. Similarly, the boxing action again can be represented with two key poses: (i) one arm is stretched and (ii) both arms are near the chest. Some of the possible poses that can be seen during walking action are shown in Figure 5 with an ID number beneath.

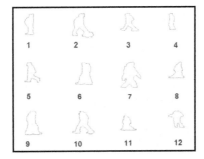

Fig. 5. Sample silhouettes from a walking sequence

The template pose database is manually created with extracted object silhouettes as shown in Figure 5 and contains key poses for all of the actions that can be recognized by the system. The pose silhouettes are labeled with integer IDs in the range [1, ID_{MAX}]. The template database which we used in our tests contains 82 poses for different actions.

5.2 Creating Action Template Database

After creating the pose database the next step is to create action templates. Actions can be represented with a histogram of key poses (pose IDs) it matches. In other words, if we create a histogram of the size of the total number of key silhouettes in the silhouette template database, and match generated silhouettes at each frame of the

Fig. 6. Sample video frames for different action types

training action sequence, to a key pose in the template silhouette database and increase the value of the corresponding bin (key pose's ID) in the histogram, we can create a histogram for the action. Formally, let $A = \{S_1, S_2, ..., S_i, ..., S_N\}$ be a sequence of silhouettes extracted from a sample motion of a human subject at each video frame $i \in [1, N]$.

Then for each S_i a corresponding pose match P_i is found in the silhouette pose template database by using the distance metric explained in Section 3.1. Let $L = \{P_1, P_2, ..., P_N\}$ represent the list of matched poses, where $P_i \in [1, ID_{MAX}]$. Then the list L can be used to create a histogram H (with ID_{MAX} bins) of IDs. After the histogram is created, it is normalized to have unit area and made ready to represent an action template like a signature. A histogram H_j is created in this manner for each action j, $j \in \{Walking, Boxing, Kicking\}$, and these histograms form the action template database. Figure 7 shows sample action histograms for each action.

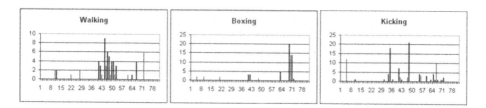

Fig. 7. Un-normalized histograms for actions in the template database

5.3   Recognizing Actions in Real-Time

After creating action template database with histograms for distinct actions, test actions are recognized in real-time.

In order to recognize an action, we keep a circular list of the IDs of the matching silhouettes in the template pose database for the subject's silhouette.

Let $A_T = \{S_{i-(w-1)}, S_{i-(w-2)}, ..., S_i\}$ be the fixed length list of the silhouettes of a test subject in the last w frames of video. For each S_i, a corresponding pose template match P_i is found in the silhouette pose template database by using the same distance metric used in training. Let $L_T = \{P_1, P_2, ..., P_N\}$ represent the list of matched pose IDs, where $P_i \in [1, ID_{MAX}]$. After this step, like in the training phase, a normalized histogram H_T of IDs is created by using the IDs in L_T.

In next step, the distance between H_T and each action template histogram H_j in the action database is calculated. The distance metric in this calculation is Euclidian distance and defined similar to the $Dist_{AB}$ as explained in Section 4.1. The action type label of the action histogram Hj, which has the minimum distance with H_T is assigned as the label of the current test action A_T. Figure 8 shows a sample history of poses for a window size of $w = 4$, in the actual implementation we use $w = 25$.

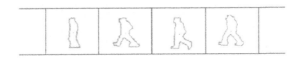

Fig. 8. Sample history window for a test sequence

6   Experimental Results

All of the tests are performed by using a video player and analyzer application that we implemented for developing our computer vision algorithms, on Microsoft Windows XP Professional operating system on a computer with an Intel PIV-2600 MHz CPU and 512 MB of RAM.

In order to test the object classification algorithm we first created a sample object template database by using an application to extract and label object silhouettes. We used four sample video clips that contain human, human group and vehicle samples. We used the template object database to classify objects in several movie clips containing human, human group and vehicle. We prepared a confusion matrix to measure the performance of our object classification algorithm. The confusion matrix is shown in Table 1. The confusion matrix is for the following object types: Human, Human Group and Vehicle.

We performed our action recognition experiments with three human subjects. One subject is used to create the template pose and template action databases and the other subjects are used in recognition tests.

Table 1. Confusion matrix for object classification

	Human	Human Group	Vehicle	Success
Human	175	13	20	84.13%
Human Group	12	52	14	66.67%
Vehicle	38	22	238	79.86%
Average Success Rate				76.88%

We created action templates for the following actions: Walking, Boxing and Kicking. Below, the confusion matrix for the cumulative action recognition results is shown:

Table 2. Confusion matrix for action recognition

	Walking	Boxing	Kicking	Success
Walking	12	1	1	85.71%
Boxing	0	4	0	100.00%
Kicking	0	1	3	75.00%
Average Success Rate				86.94%

7 Discussion

In this paper, we proposed a novel system for real-time object classification and human action recognition using object silhouettes. The test results show that the presented method is promising and can be improved with some further work to reduce false alarms. The proposed methods can also be utilized as part of a multimedia database to extract useful facts from video clips [19].

A weakness of the proposed methods is that they are view dependent. If the camera setup is different in training and testing, the success rate will be too low. Automating the template database creation steps will help to obtain a self calibrating object classification and human action recognition system.

Acknowledgement

This work is supported in part by European Commission Sixth Framework Program with Grant No: 507752 (MUSCLE Network of Excellence Project).

References

[1] J.K. Aggarwal and Q. Cai. Human motion analysis: a review. Computer Vision and Image Understanding, 73(3):428–440, March 1999.

[2] E. M. Arkin, L.P. Chew, D.P. Huttenlocher, K. Kedem, and J.S.B. Mitchell. An efficiently computable metric for comparing polygonal shapes. IEEE Transactions on Pattern Recognition and Machine Intelligence, 13:209–216, 1991.

[3] A. Enis Cetin, Report on progress with respect to partial solutions on human detection algorithms, human activity analysis methods, and multimedia databases. WP-11 Report, EU FP6-NoE: MUSCLE (Multimedia Understanding Through Computation and Semantics), www.muscle-noe.org, May 2005.

[4] O. Chomat, J.L. Crowley, Recognizing motion using local appearance, International Symposium on Intelligent Robotic Systems, University of Edinburgh, pages 271-279, 1998.

[5] R. T. Collins, R. Gross, and J. Shi. Silhouette-based human identification from body shape and gait. In Proc. of Fifth IEEE Conf. on Automatic Face and Gesture Recognition, pages 366–371, 2002.

[6] R. Cutler and L.S. Davis. Robust real-time periodic motion detection, analysis and applications. IEEE Transactions on Pattern Analysis and Machine Intelligence, 8:781–796, 2000.

[7] R. T. Collins et al. A system for video surveillance and monitoring: VSAM final report. Technical report CMU-RI-TR-00-12, Robotics Institute, Carnegie Mellon University, May 2000.

[8] Y. Dedeoglu, Moving object detection, tracking and classification for smart video surveillance, Master's Thesis, Dept. of Computer Eng. Bilkent University, Ankara, 2004.

[9] D. M. Gavrila. The analysis of human motion and its application for visual surveillance. In Proc. of the 2nd IEEE International Workshop on Visual Surveillance, pages 3–5, Fort Collins, U.S.A., 1999.

[10] I. Haritaoglu, D. Harwood, and L.S. Davis. W4: A real time system for detecting and tracking people. In Computer Vision and Pattern Recognition, pages 962–967, 1998.

[11] F. Heijden. Image based measurement systems: object recognition and parameter estimation. Wiley, January 1996.

[12] J. Heikkila and O. Silven. A real-time system for monitoring of cyclists and pedestrians. In Proc. of Second IEEE Workshop on Visual Surveillance, pages 74–81, Fort Collins, Colorado, June 1999.

[13] H.Ramoser, T.Schlgl, M.Winter, and H.Bischof. Shape-based detection of humans for video surveillance. In Proc. of IEEE Int. Conf. on Image Processing, pages 1013-1016, Barcelona, Spain, 2003.

[14] A. J. Lipton. Local application of optic flow to analyse rigid versus non-rigid motion. Technical Report CMU-RI-TR-99-13, Robotics Institute, Carnegie Mellon University, Pittsburgh, PA, December 1999.

[15] A. J. Lipton, H. Fujiyoshi, and R.S. Patil. Moving target classification and tracking from real-time video. In Proc. of Workshop Applications of Computer Vision, pages 129–136, 1998.

[16] S. Loncaric. A survey of shape analysis techniques. Pattern Recognition, 31(8):983–1001, August 1998.

[17] A. M. McIvor. Background subtraction techniques. In Proc. of Image and Vision Computing, Auckland, New Zealand, 2000.

[18] E. Saykol, U. Gudukbay, and O. Ulusoy. A histogram-based approach for object-based query-by-shape-and-color in multimedia databases, Image and Vision Computing, vol. 23, No. 13, pages 1170-1180, November 2005.

[19] E. Saykol, U. Gudukbay, O. Ulusoy. A Database Model for Querying Visual Surveillance by Integrating Semantic and Low-Level Features. In Lecture Notes in Computer Science (LNCS), (Proc. of 11th International Workshop on Multimedia Information Systems-MIS'05), Vol. 3665, pages 163-176, Edited by K. S. Candan and A. Celentano, Sorrento, Italy, September 2005.

[20] E. Saykol, G. Gulesir, U. Gudukbay, and O. Ulusoy. KiMPA: A kinematics-based method for polygon approximation. In Lecture Notes in Computer Science (LNCS), Vol. 2457, pages 186-194, Advances in Information Sciences (ADVIS'2002) Edited by Tatyana Yakhno, Springer-Verlag, 2002.

[21] C. Schuldt, I. Laptev and B. Caputo, Recognizing human actions: a local SVM approach, In Proc. of ICPR'04, Cambridge, UK.

[22] C. Stauffer and W. Grimson. Adaptive background mixture models for realtime tracking. In Proc. of the IEEE Computer Society Conference on Computer Vision and Pattern Recognition, pages 246-252, 1999.

[23] B. U. Toreyin, A. E. Cetin, A. Aksay, M. B. Akhan, Moving object detection in wavelet compressed video. Signal Processing: Image Communication, EURASIP, Elsevier, vol. 20, pages 255-265, 2005.

[24] B. U. Toreyin, Y. Dedeoglu, A. E. Cetin, HMM based falling person detection using both audio and video. IEEE International Workshop on Human-Computer Interaction, Beijing, China, Oct. 21, 2005 (in conjunction with ICCV 2005), Lecture Notes in Computer Science, vol. 3766, pages 211-220, Springer-Verlag GmbH, 2005.

[25] R.C. Veltkamp and M. Hagedoorn. State-of-the-art in shape matching, In Principles of Visual Information Retrieval, pages 87–119, Springer, 2001.

[26] L. Wang, W. Hu, and T. Tan. Recent developments in human motion analysis. Pattern Recognition, 36(3):585–601, March 2003.

[27] L. Wixson and A. Selinger. Classifying moving objects as rigid or non-rigid. In Proc. of DARPA Image Understanding Workshop, pages 341–358, 1998.

Voice Activity Detection Using Wavelet-Based Multiresolution Spectrum and Support Vector Machines and Audio Mixing Algorithm

Wei Xue, Sidan Du, Chengzhi Fang, and Yingxian Ye

Department of Electronics Science and Engineering,
Nanjing University,
Nanjing 210093, P.R. China
xwsky2008@hotmail.com,
coff128@nju.edu.cn

Abstract. This paper presents a Voice Activity Detection (VAD) algorithm and efficient speech mixing algorithm for a multimedia conference. The proposed VAD uses MFCC of multiresolution spectrum based on wavelets and two classical audio parameters as audio feature, and prejudges silence by detection of multi-gate zero cross ratio, and classify noise and voice by Support Vector Machines (SVM). New speech mixing algorithm used in Multipoint Control Unit (MCU) of conferences imposes short-time power of each audio stream as mixing weight vector, and is designed for parallel processing in program. Various experiments show, proposed VAD algorithm achieves overall better performance in all SNRs than VAD of G.729b and other VAD, output audio of new speech mixing algorithm has excellent hearing perceptibility, and its computational time delay are small enough to satisfy the needs of real-time transmission, and MCU computation is lower than that based on G.729b VAD.

1 Introduction

Voice activity detection and audio mixing are important techniques in the area of the network speech communication platform. For a wide range of applications such as GSM, Video Meeting, Network Phone, with the use of VAD, system computation load is reduced and network bandwidth is saved. In early VAD algorithms, the VAD determine the silence by comparing the extracted audio features with the initialized threshold. Parameters include short-time zero-crossing, short-time energy, autocorrelation coefficients, LPC [1]-[3]. Because background noise signal is volatile and algorithm uses fixed threshold for comparison, systems adopting these parameters as features perform not well especially in noisy environments.

Papers [4]-[6] suggest using subband or wavelet filters to decompose the audio data, and extract parameters in various frequency. Because of the energy leak of the filter, it is difficult to get the whole frequency spectrum of the signal from the subsection of frequency spectrum. And existing VAD techniques (GSM [7]、 G.729B [8], etc.) misjudge part of air stream noise as normal voice. In order to overcome these

T.S. Huang et al. (Eds.): HCI/ECCV 2006, LNCS 3979, pp. 78–88, 2006.

problems, we present audio MFCC [9] feature of wavelets-based multiresolution spectrum (WBMS) representing the whole frequency spectrum of the signal, and classify voice by SVM with MFCC of WBMS.

Speaking by more than two users at the same time is allowed in speech communication system, the audio mixing techniques should be introduced. Computer has limited ability to describe the range of sound intensity. Adopting linear superposition as the algorithm of speech mixing in computer, just like what is done in nature, will inevitably cause overflow of superposition [10]. And new noise could be added to output audio by mixing algorithm in [11]. To overcome these defects, the paper presents a new method, adaptive-weighted (AW) algorithm.

The paper is organized as follows. In section 2, we describe communication system framework integrated with voice activity detection and sound mixer. In section 3, we present voice activity detection algorithm including audio feature extraction, silence detection of multi-gate zero cross ratio, SVM theory and VAD algorithm. In section 4, we introduce speech mixing algorithm. Then, section 5 shows experiments on VAD and speech mixing algorithm, and MCU performance. Finally, section 6 gives conclusions.

2 Communication System Integrated with Voice Activity Detection and Sound Mixer

The communication system introduces two new algorithms: voice activity detection of audio sending client, real-time sound mixer of MCU.

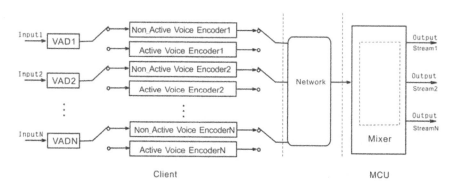

Fig. 1. Proposed communication system framework

The system adopts the centralized communication architecture [12]. According to that, sound mixer processes audio streams in MCU. Audio mixer unit obtains audio streams from every client and sends back to the clients after mixing them. It helps torelease the network communication burden and reduce the computation of every receiving client.

3   Voice Activity Detection

In communication systems based on the agreement such as G.729B, G.723.1A, etc., when the speaker does not speak and there is no obvious noise around, there are still audio frames sent. It shows that the weaker background sound could be judged as the normal voice. For example, the signals of the breath air stream caused by the nose or the mouth near the microphone. So we propose new VAD using detection of multi-gate zero cross ratio and SVM [13] to distinguish the background sound including air stream noise (fake voice) and other background noise from normal voice. In the paper, the sound is divided into three kinds: real silence (background noise), fake voice and normal voice.

3.1   Audio Feature Parameters Extraction

The parameters include two parts: feeling features, MFCC of wavelets-based multiresolution spectrum.

1) Feeling features
    Z_{ci}: Z_{ci} is the zero cross ratio of frame i.
    E_i : E_i is the short-time energy value of frame i.

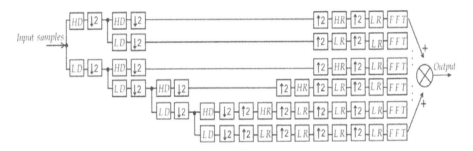

Fig. 2. Direct computation of WBMS

2) MFCC of WBMS
    We uses Daubechies4 wavelets [14] to decompose the data into N sub-band, and reconstructs sub-bands to the size the same as that after the first wavelets decomposition, and normalizes each sub-band coefficients, and makes FFT transformation to them. After these, we sum up all the sub-band coefficients altogether to produce WBMS, and then extract MFCC from WBMS.
    Suppose LD, HD, LR, HR as the decomposition low-pass filter, decomposition high-pass filter, reconstruction low-pass filter, and reconstruction high-pass filter of wavelets. ↓2 is extraction operator, which extracts the even subscript parts of the original series to produce a new series. ↑2 is filling operator, which inserts a zero in the original series every two points.

MFCC parameters are:

$$c_{MFCC}(i) = \sqrt{\frac{2}{L}} \sum_{l=1}^{L} \log m(l) \cos\left\{(l - \frac{1}{2})\frac{i\pi}{L}\right\} \tag{1}$$

In the equation (1),

$$m(l) = \sum_{k=o(l)}^{h(l)} W_l(k)|X_n(k)| \quad ,l = 1,2,...,L \tag{2}$$

$$W_l(k) = \begin{cases} \dfrac{k - o(l)}{c(l) - o(l)} & o(l) \leq k \leq c(l) \\ \dfrac{h(l) - k}{h(l) - c(l)} & c(l) \leq k \leq h(l) \end{cases} \tag{3}$$

Where o(l), c(l) and h(l) is the lower limit, central limit and upper limit frequency of a triangle filter, X(k) is WBMS.

3.2 Real Silence Detection of Multi-gate Zero Cross Ratio

We introduce multi-gate zero cross ratio [15] to prejudge the real silence. Suppose three different thresholds, $T_1 < T_2 < T_3$. For every frame, we use equation (4) to compute three multi-gate zero cross ratio Z_1, Z_2, Z_3 with T_1, T_2, T_3.

$$Z_n = \sum\left\{\left|sgn[x(n) - T_n] - sgn[x(n-1) - T_n]\right| + \left|sgn[x(n) + T_n] - sgn[x(n-1) + T_n]\right|\right\} \tag{4}$$

$$* w(n - w)$$

The weighted sum denotes the total zero cross ratio.

$$Z = W_1Z_1 + W_2Z_2 + W_3Z_3$$

Where W_1, W_2, W_3 is zero cross weight. Z is the sum of zero cross ratio, which is called weighted sum for short.

By selecting the threshold and weight value properly, we can make the Z of normal voice become obviously larger than that of the silence. Z_0 is defined as the threshold of weighted sum.

When $Z > Z_0$, it is judged as voice frame, otherwise, as silence frame.

3.3 Support Vector Machines

The basic theory of the two classification SVM is, maping the input space to another space (feature space) using non-linear transformation, then seeking the optimal linear classification plane of the samples in this new space (maximizing the classification interval of the two class samples). The non-linear transformation is realized by defining proper inner product function (or kernel function). The two sample classes mentioned above nearest to the optimal classification plane, is called support vector (SV).

Suppose two dividable sample sets (x_i, y_i), $i=1,2, \ldots, n$, $x_i = [x_i^1, x_i^2, \ldots, x_i^d]^T$, $x_i \in R^d$, $y_i \in \{+1, -1\}$ is class maker. Optimal classification plane function is:

$$g(x_i) = \sum_{j=1}^{n} a_j^{op} y_j K(x_i, x_j) + b^{op}, \quad i=1,2,\cdots,n \tag{5}$$

Where b^{op} is classification threshold, $K(x_i, y_i)$ is a inner product function. Here we select the radial basis function below as the inner product function. Such SVM is a radial basis function classification machine (in experiment, $\sigma^2 = 0.3$).

$$K(x_i, x_j) = \exp\left(-\frac{\| x_i - x_j \|^2}{\sigma^2}\right) \tag{6}$$

Optimal classification plane function is decided by the optimal results of the function $Q(a)$ below.

$$\underset{a}{Min} \quad Q(a) = -\sum_{i=1}^{n} a_i + 0.5 \sum_{i=1}^{n}\sum_{j=1}^{n} a_i a_j y_i y_j K(x_i, x_j) \tag{7}$$

$$Subject \quad to \quad \sum_{i=1}^{n} y_i a_i = 0, \quad c \geq a_i \geq 0, \quad i = 1,2,\cdots,n$$

Where c is a constant. Equation (7) is a quadratic function under inequality constraint, exclusive optimal answer exists. According to the conditions Kühn-Tucker, among the optimal value of Q(a), most a_i^{op} is 0. When the a_i^{op} is unequal to 0 (denotes a_i^{sv}, $i=1, 2,\ldots, s$), x_i^{sv} is support vector, $i=1, 2, \ldots, s$, and y_i^{sv} is class marker of x_i^{sv}, b^{op} can be worked out in equation (8).

$$b^{op} = y_i^{sv} - \sum_{j=1}^{n} a_j^{op} y_j K(x_i^{sv}, x_j) = y_i^{sv} - \sum_{j=1}^{s} a_j^{sv} y_j^{sv} K(x_i^{sv}, x_j^{sv}) \tag{8}$$

We get the optimal classification function of SVM in equation (9).

$$f(x) = sign\{g(x)\} = sign\left(\sum_{j=1}^{n} a_j^{op} y_j K(x, x_j) + b^{op}\right) = sign\left(\sum_{i=1}^{s} a_i^{sv} y_i^{sv} K(x, x_i^{sv}) + b^{op}\right) \tag{9}$$

Where sign (.) is a sign function.

3.4 Algorithm of Voice Activity Detection

Algorithm extracts audio feature parameters from voice frame, and detects the real silence by multi-gate zero cross ratio. If $Z < Z_0$, the frame is judged as real silence, and is filled with self-adaptive noise produced by the CNG of G.729B. Otherwise, the voice data will be classified by SVM into the normal voice and background sound including the fake voice or misjudged real silence. If the background sound is detected, the frame would be filled with self-adaptive noise.

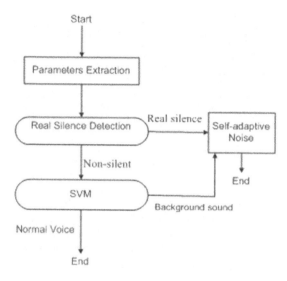

Fig. 3. Voice Activity Detection Algorithm

4 Real-Time Audio Mixing

New algorithm aims at decreasing volume decline of mixed voice data and reducing the spectrum diffused effect of the original signals by slowing down the varying speed of the weight series used by mixer. Define w[j] as weight, which varies only one time during 10 frames, or 0.1s. According to the sampling theory, if effective bandwidth of a series with only 10 samples per second is less than 5Hz, spectrum diffusion can be restricted in the range of ±10 Hz.

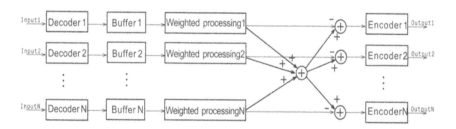

Fig. 4. The principle of speech mixing in MCU

The average value of each audio stream in the ten frames is worked out.

$$Avg[j] = \frac{1}{10l} \sum_{i=0}^{10l-1} |data[j,i]| \tag{10}$$

Where data[j,i] in the equation (10) denotes the No i sample in the No j audio stream. L is the number of voice samples in a frame. The weight of No j voice stream is computed in equation (11).

$$w[j] = Avg[j] \bigg/ \sum_{p=0}^{n-1} Avg[j] \qquad (11)$$

And then do speech mixing in the equation (12).

$$MixData[i] = \sum_{j=0}^{n-1} data[j,i] * w[j] \qquad (12)$$

$$\sum_{j=0}^{n-1} w[j] = 1 \qquad (13)$$

Because the computing of Avg[j] of every stream in fig. 4 is independent to each other, each stream can be computed in parallel. This situation continues until reaching the step of speech mixing. So the algorithm is designed into high parallel computing structure, and uses the MMX/SSE/SSE2 instruction set for optimization.

5 Experimental Results

Experiments on VAD compare the proposed VAD with G.729b VAD and MFCC+SVM [4] VAD in terms of probability of detecting speech frames. Experiments on new real-time speech mixing algorithm emphasizes on evaluating the output audio waveform and hearing perceptibility, and how long the speech mixing program consumes when multiple voice streams are being decoded, mixed and encoded in mixer. And MCU performance of video conference system using proposed VAD and new speech mixing algorithm is tested.

Audio signal is sampled at 8kHz and a frame is of 80 samples, each frame continues 10ms. All the data for training and testing SVM of voice activity detection is from database "Aurora". These sets of data are separately added actually noise or breathing sound. We collected 20 voice samples (60s per sample) for speech mixing test.

5.1 Experiments on New VAD

Multi-gate zero cross ratio for VAD needs optimal weight vectors. We build the target function based on ratio of the incorrect decision to real silence, and traverse each of the weight vector and the threshold value to find out the optimal weight vector and threshold value with lowest ratio of the incorrect decision.

Audio features consist of two parts: two feeling features and L=12 MFCC of WBMS. We adopt SMO [16] algorithm for SVM training. P_d is the probability of correctly detecting normal voice. P_s is the probability of correctly detecting fake noise. P_c is the probability of incorrectly detecting real silence (not including the fake voice). P_f is the probability of correctly detecting silence (including the fake voice and real silence) for the G.729B algorithm.

The results show that the proposed VAD has an overall better performance than MFCC+SVM VAD, G.729B VAD in all SNRs and the noise types used here, as evident by a lower probability of false detection and a higher probability of correct

Table 1. Comparison of the proposed VAD with the MFCC+SVM VAD and G.729B VAD in terms of probability of detecting speech frames for conference noise, MFCC + SVM VAD prejudges real silence by Multi-gate zero cross ratio detection

Noise type	SNR (db)	Proposed VAD			MFCC + SVM VAD			G.729B VAD	
		$P_s(\%)$	$P_s(\%)$	$P_f(\%)$	$P_s(\%)$	$P_s(\%)$	$P_f(\%)$	$P_s(\%)$	$P_f(\%)$
White	25	99.81	95.32	1.48	99.72	88.92	2.36	99.77	16.30
	15	98.47	89.18	2.18	97.43	85.17	3.45	96.61	23.86
	5	94.63	50.28	2.52	91.28	38.48	4.16	85.05	36.75
Conference	25	99.71	93.45	1.72	99.61	87.44	2.52	99.53	19.42
	15	98.26	90.36	2.25	97.27	84.53	3.65	95.76	27.57
	5	93.52	52.63	3.12	90.56	38.23	4.28	84.56	41.83

speech detection. While SNR declining, P_s of proposed VAD has a high fall, but could be above 50%. And high P_f shows G.729B can't efficiently detect fake voice.

5.2 Experiments on New Speech Mixing Algorithm

To analyze the output audio waveform after speech mixing and evaluate hearing feeling, we implement speech mixing algorithm on two audio streams. In fig. 5 (a)-(c), the waveform of mixed result seems the superposition of input streams waveforms, and fig. 5 (d) is similar to (c). In the experiment on hearing perceptibility, the output of AW is superior to that of ASW [17]. Output of AW is smooth and has no plosive and discontinuous sound. Output of ASW has continuous noise, because the weights used in speech mixing varies with the time, and is random, spectrum of output appears too dispersive after speech mixing, and when it comes to 4 mixing streams,

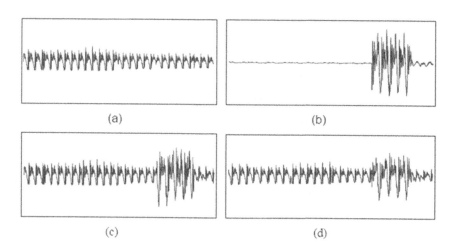

(a)

(b)

(c)

(d)

Fig. 5. Mixing result in time-domain ((a), (b) are input audio waveforms in time domain, (c) is output of AW, and (d) is output of ASW)

experiment shows output involves more noise and sounds discontinuous to distinguish the each voice of speaker.

We test how long the mixing program consumes in processing different number streams. In experiments, every stream lasts 60s. Respectively mix the 3-20 audio streams, and decode and encode them by G.729A, results are the mixing time of different number streams. When 20 streams are mixing, the computer's CPU occupation rate is less than 5%.

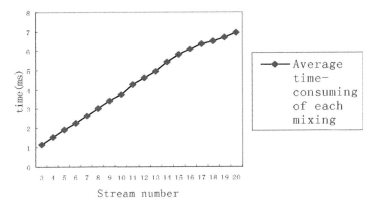

Fig. 6. Time-consuming of different number streams in AW speech mixing (Program runs on a P4 CPU, 512M memory computer)

5.3 Experiments on MCU Performance

We have developed a video conference system using proposed VAD and speech mixing algorithm. For 3-10 conference clients, we respectively calculate the average value of mixed audio streams number of each mixing process of MCU in 20 minutes.

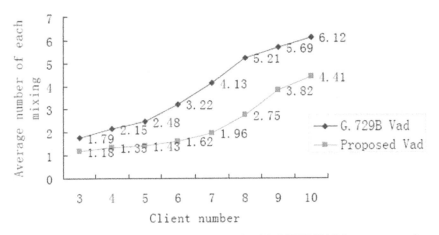

Fig. 7. Comparison of MCU using the proposed VAD with G.729B VAD in average number of mixing streams of each mixing

Fig. 7 shows that the average number of mixing streams of system using proposed VAD, is less than that using G.729B VAD. Because of the high correct decision ratio of proposed VAD, the number of audio data transmitted to MCU decreases, and computation of the MCU declines. System allows more clients to attend the audio discussion in same hardware conditions than that using G.729B.

6 Conclusions

We presents a centralized speech mixing system framework combined with new voice activity detection and new speech mixing algorithm. In the new voice activity detection algorithm, we use MFCC of WBMS and two feeling parameters as the audio features. In order to distinguish the normal voice from the fake voice and real silence, we use the multi-gate zero cross ratio to prejudge the real silence, and complete the voice activity detection by SVM. Compared with the VAD algorithm in the G.729B and the VAD with MFCC+SVM, the proposed VAD algorithm achieves high correct decision ratio of voice in various SNR.

As the important technique of the MCU, AW algorithm is introduced to mix audio streams. Hearing perceptibility test performs well. And the algorithm is designed into high parallel computing structure. For the 20 streams speech mixing, its computational time delay is small and CPU occupation rate is low, the performance of MCU satisfies the needs of real-time transmission. When the video conference system uses the new voice activity detection and AW speech mixing algorithm, speech mixing computation of MCU is much less than that of conference system using G.729B VAD. The same hardware conditions allow more clients to connect MCU and take part in the voice discussion.

References

1. Nemer, E., Goubran, R, Mahmoud, S.: Robust voice activity detection using higher-order statistics in the LPC residual domain. IEEE Transactions on Speech and Audio Processing, vol. 9, March (2001) 217-231
2. J. C. Junqua, B. Reaves, and B. Mak: A study of endpoint detection algorithms in adverse conditions: Incidence on a DTW and HMM recognize. In Proc. Eurospeech'91, (1991) 371-1374
3. A. Sangwan, M. C. Chiranth, H. S. Jamadagni, R. Sah, R. V. Prasad, and V. Gaurav: VAD techniques for real-time speech transmission on the Internet. In IEEE International Conference on High-Speed Networks and Multimedia Communications, (2002) 46-50
4. Guodong Guo, Stan Z. Li: Content-Based Audio Classificationand Retrieval by Support VectorMachines. IEEE Trans. on Neural Networks, vol. 14, no. 1, January (2003) 209-215
5. J. Stegmann, G. Schroeder: Robust Voice Activity Detection Based on the Wavelet Transform. Proc. IEEE Workshop on Speech Coding, September 7-10, (1997) 99-100
6. Chien-Chang Lin, Shi-Huang Chen, T. K. Truong, and Yukon Chang: Audio Classification and Categorization Based on Wavelets and Support Vector Machine. IEEE Transactions on Speech and Audio Processing, vol. 13, no. 5, Sept. (2005) 644-651
7. ETSI: Draft Recommendation prETS 300 724: GSM Enhanced Full Rate (EFR) speech codec, (1996)

8. ITU-T: Draft Recommendation G.729, Annex B: Voice Activity Detection (1996)
9. L. Rabiner and B. H. Juang: Fundamentals of Speech Recognition. Englewood Cliffs, NJ: Prentice-Hall (1993)
10. Agustín JG, Hussein AW: Audio mixing for interactive multimedia communications. JCIS'98, Research Triangle, NC, (1998) 217-220
11. Shutang Yang, Shengsheng Yu, Jingli Zhou: Multipoint communications with speech mixing over IP network. Computer communications, vol. 25, (2002) 46-55
12. Venkat RP, Harrick MV, Srinivas R: Communication architectures and algorithms for media mixing in multimedia conferences. IEEE/ACM Trans. on Networking, vol. 1, no. 1, (1993) 20-30
13. Cortes C, Vapnik C. Support Vector Networks. Machine Learning, vol. 20, (1995) 273-297
14. Daubechies, I., Ten Lectures on Wavelets, SIAM, Philadelphia (1992)
15. Thomas Parsons W.: Voice and Speech Processing. McGraw-Hill Book Company (1986)
16. JOHN C. PLATT: A Fast Algorithm for Training Support Vector Machines. Microsoft Research Technical Report MSR-TR-98-14, April (1998)
17. Fan Xing, Gu Wei-kang: Research on fast real-time adaptive audio mixing in multimedia conference. Journal of Zhejiang University Science, vol 6a, no.6, May (2005) 507-512

Action Recognition in Broadcast Tennis Video Using Optical Flow and Support Vector Machine

Guangyu Zhu[1], Changsheng Xu[2], Wen Gao[1,3], and Qingming Huang[3]

[1] Harbin Institute of Technology, Harbin, P.R. China
[2] Institute for Infocomm Research, 21 Heng Mui Keng Terrace, Singapore
[3] Graduate School of Chinese Academy of Sciences, Beijing, P.R. China
{gyzhu, wgao, qmhuang}@jdl.ac.cn,
xucs@i2r.a-star.edu.sg

Abstract. Motion analysis in broadcast sports video is a challenging problem especially for player action recognition due to the low resolution of players in the frames. In this paper, we present a novel approach to recognize the basic player actions in broadcast tennis video where the player is about 30 pixels tall. Two research challenges, motion representation and action recognition, are addressed. A new motion descriptor, which is a group of histograms based on optical flow, is proposed for motion representation. The optical flow here is treated as spatial pattern of noisy measurement instead of precise pixel displacement. To recognize the action performed by the player, support vector machine is employed to train the classifier where the concatenation of histograms is formed as the input features. Experimental results demonstrate that our method is promising by integrating with the framework of multimodal analysis in sports video.

1 Introduction

The motion or action performed by players in tennis game can reveal the process of the game and the tactics of the players. It is essential for analysis of the matches and desired for sports professionals and longtime fanners for technical coaching assistant and tactics analysis.

Considering the appearance ratio of playfield in one frame shown in Fig. 1, the frames/shots of broadcast tennis video can be divided into two classes: close-up view where the magnitude of player figure is higher, and far-view where the magnitude is lower. In close-up, a player figure is usually 300 pixels tall. It is easy to segment and label human body parts such as the limbs, torso, and head resulting in marking out a stick figure. Existing work [1][2] has achieved good results on action recognition for close-up view. On the other hand, in far-view frame, a player figure might be only 30 pixels tall. The action detail of the player is blurred due to the low figure resolution. In this case, we can only track the player as a blob and extract the spatial translation. It is very difficult to articulate the separate movements of different body parts. Thus we cannot discriminate among too many action categories for the far-view video. To the best of our knowledge, there are few efforts devoted in the research of tennis player action

T.S. Huang et al. (Eds.): HCI/ECCV 2006, LNCS 3979, pp. 89–98, 2006.

Fig. 1. Two typical frames derived from broadcast tennis video. (a) Close-up scene, (b) Far-view scene, the zoomed picture is the player whose action to be recognized.

recognition in broadcast video. Miyamori and Iisaku [3] developed an automatic annotation system of tennis actions including foreside-swing, backside-swing and over-the-shoulder swing. The analysis is based on silhouette transitions. However, appearance is not necessarily preserved across different sequences and less robust for classification. Compared with action recognition for the videos with high resolution figures, a little work [4][5] is attempting to analyze poor quality, non-stationary camera footage. The approach proposed in [4] modeled the structure of the appearance self-similarity matrix and was able to handle very small objects. Unfortunately, this method was based on periodicity and thus restricted to periodic motion. Efros *et al.* [5] developed a generic approach to recognize actions in "medium field" which is similar to "far-view" defined in this paper. In their paper, a motion descriptor based on optical flow in a spatio-temporal volume was introduced and an associated similarity measure was utilized in a nearest neighbor classification (NNC) framework to perform action categorization. The experimental results on tennis data set are promising. However, the videos they used are non-broadcast which has less challenge for tracking and recognition.

In this paper, we propose a novel motion analysis approach to recognize the player actions in far-view of the broadcast tennis video. Fig. 2 shows the flow diagram. Our method starts by tracking and stabilizing player figure in each frame. In [3][5], the template based and normalized-correlation based tracker were utilized. By our observations, however, these algorithms are not robust enough for long time player tracking in the broadcast video. A sophisticated tracking strategy called SVR particle filter [6], which is an improved particle filter, is employed in our method. Optical flow field is derived as low-level feature with the post-processing of half-wave rectification and Gaussian smoothing. The optical flow field is then divided into slices based on the relationship between locomotory body parts and figure regions. Slice based optical flow histograms, which is a new motion descriptor henceforth abbreviated as S-OFHs, is proposed to provide a compact representation for spatial pattern of noisy optical flow. The concatenation of S-OFHs is fed into support vector machine learning framework to robustly capture the discriminative patterns in S-OFHs space. Two basic actions, left-swing and right-swing, are recognized in our experiments.

The rest of the paper is organized as follows. Section 2 introduces the player tracking and stabilizing module. In section 3, the local motion descriptor, which is slice based optical flow histograms, is proposed. Section 4 describes the

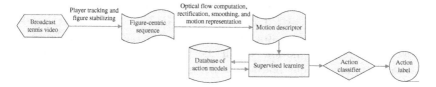

Fig. 2. Flow diagram of action recognition approach

classification mechanism based on support vector machine. Experimental results are presented and analyzed in section 5. Finally, we conclude the paper with future work in section 6.

2   Player Tracking and Stabilization

Our recognition algorithm starts by player tracking and human-centric figure computation. This can be achieved by tracking the player candidate region and then constructing a window in each frame centered at the player region.

The appropriate trackers utilized in our method are required to be consistent, that is, the tracker should be robust enough for the noisy circumstance so as to always map the person in a particular body configuration to approximately the same stabilized image. Existing methods for tracking tennis players are based on template matching [3][7][8] which is similar to the correlation based algorithm in [5]. These trackers are sensitive to the noise such as player deformation and background clutter caused by non-rigid object and low frame resolution, and cannot track player for a long video sequence. This can be exemplified in [7] that the input tennis video was first segmented into chunks of 30 frames and then performed tracking for each chunk separately. A sophisticated tracking strategy called SVR particle filter is employed in our approach. SVR particle filter enhances the performance of classical particle filter with small sample set and is robust enough for the noise in broadcast video. The experimental result is very satisfying. More details about this tracker can be found in [6].

To derive the human-centric figure, the tracking window around the player region is then enlarged by a certain scale in pixel unit and a simple method of computing centroid of the player region is used. The centroid coordinates of the region are defined as follows:

$$m_x = \frac{\sum_{x \in R} \sum_{y \in R} x f(x, y)}{\sum_{x \in R} \sum_{y \in R} f(x, y)} . \tag{1}$$

$$m_y = \frac{\sum_{x \in R} \sum_{y \in R} y f(x, y)}{\sum_{x \in R} \sum_{y \in R} f(x, y)} . \tag{2}$$

where R is the region occupied by the object on the image plane and $f(x, y)$ the gray level at location (x, y). Then the center of window controlled by tracker is shifted to position (m_x, m_y).

Once the video sequence is stabilized, the motion in broadcast video caused by camera behavior can be treated as being removed. This corresponds to a skillful movement by a camera operator who keeps the moving figure in the center of the view. Any residual motion within the human-centric figure is due to the relative motion of different body parts as limbs, head, torso and racket played with player.

3   Motion Descriptor Computation

As mentioned above, in previous approaches, appearance is not necessarily preserved across different action sequences. Different players may exhibit different postures for the same action and different postures may be recorded in different video even for the same action. Thus the appearance descriptor is not robust and discriminative for action recognition and classification.

We derive our features on pixel-wise optical flow as it is the most intuitive technique for capturing motion independent of appearance. The key challenge is that the computation of optical flow is not very accurate, particularly on coarse and noisy data such as broadcast video footage. The essence of our approach is to treat optical flow field as spatial pattern of noisy measurements which are aggregated using our motion descriptor instead of precise pixel displacements at points. Within the human-centric figure, the motion is due to the relative movements caused by player's different body parts which are the different regions being mapped into the image plane. These motion characteristics cannot be captured well by global features computed from the whole figure. A simple means of localizing the motion for recognition is to separately pay attention to different regions around the human torso. One way of doing this is to divide the optical flow field into various sub-regions called slices here. The histogram is utilized to represent the spatial distribution for each sub optical flow field in slices.

3.1   Optical Flow Computation and Noise Elimination

Before computing the motion descriptor, the optical flow feature of human-centric figure is derived and the noise in the flow field is eliminated by the algorithm shown in Fig. 3.

Noise in the background of human-centric figure makes significant influence for the computation of optical flow inside the human region. It necessitates background subtraction before computing optical flow. Considering the background of human-centric figure is playfield, an adaptive method of playfield detection [9] is applied in our experiments. After background pixel detection, region growing technique in [10] is performed as the post-processing to connect background pixels into regions, eliminate noises, and smooth boundaries.

We compute optical flow at each figure using Horn-Schunck algorithm [11]. The half-wave rectification and Gaussian smoothing is performed to eliminate the noise in optical flow field. The optical flow magnitudes are first thresholded to reduce the effect of too small and too large motion probably due to noise

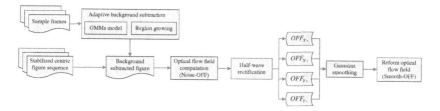

Fig. 3. Optical flow computation and noise elimination

inside the human region. The optical flow vector field OFF is then split into two scalar fields corresponding to the horizontal and vertical components OFF_X and OFF_Y, each of which is then half-wave rectified into four non-negative channels OFF_X^+, OFF_X^-, OFF_Y^+, and OFF_Y^-, so that $OFF_X = OFF_X^+ - OFF_X^-$ and $OFF_Y = OFF_Y^+ - OFF_Y^-$. They are each smoothed with a Gaussian filter to obtain the final channels. The smoothed optical flow field is reformed finally.

3.2   Local Motion Representation

Motion representation with global methods takes the whole image or video sequence into account. Local methods, on the other hand, focus on certain parts of the image or video data.

With the context of action recognition, the motion in the human-centric figure is due to the relative movement of different body parts which are exhibited in the different figure regions. This can be demonstrated by observing the optical flow field computed from the processed human-centric figure (see Fig. 4(a)). For left-swing, the optical flow field in left figure region is much denser than the field in right region. Contrarily, the field in the right region is denser than that in left region for right-swing. By this observation, we adopt a simple but effective region style which is called as slice. The whole optical flow field is split into three slices along the width orientation as show in Fig. 4(b). The height of the slice is equal to the one of figure and the width can be set adaptively in accordance with the object spatial structure. Here, we set even width for each slice.

Histogram based methods are widely used for spatial recognition. The advantage of histogram based representation is that it provides much information using very compact description if the dimensionality of the histogram is low. Motivated by the kernel density estimation for color distribution [12], a group of slice based optical flow histograms (S-OFHs) are derived. First we define $b(\mathbf{p}) \in \{1, \ldots, m\}$ as as the bin index of histogram associated with the optical flow vector $\mathbf{f}$ at location $\mathbf{p}$. For each position $\mathbf{q}$ inside optical flow field OFF, considering a grid region $R(\mathbf{q})$ centered at $\mathbf{q}$, the probability of the bin $u = 1, \ldots, m$ in the histogram of OFF is then computed as

$$h_u = C \sum_{\mathbf{q} \in OFF} \sum_{\mathbf{p} \in R(\mathbf{q})} k(\|\mathbf{p} - \mathbf{q}\|)\delta[b(\mathbf{p}) - u] \, . \tag{3}$$

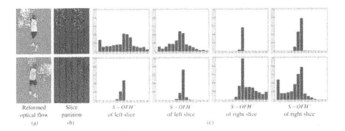

Fig. 4. Slice partition and slice based optical flow histograms (S-OFHs) of left and right swing

where δ is the Kronecker delta function, C is the normalization constant ensuring $\sum_{u=1}^{m} h_u = 1$, k is a convex and monotonic decreasing kernel profile which assigns a smaller weight to the locations that are farther from the center $\mathbf{q}$.

Given an optical flow field OFF_i for the figure F_i in human-centric figure sequence, $i = 1, \ldots, N$, where N is the total figure number, $OFF_{i,j}$ is the sub optical flow field in the jth slice, $j = 1, \ldots, L$ and here $L = 3$, the $S - OFH_{i,j}$ is then defined as follows accroding to Eq. 3:

$$h_u^{i,j} = C \sum_{\mathbf{q} \in OFF_{i,j}} \sum_{\mathbf{p} \in R(\mathbf{q})} k(\|\mathbf{p} - \mathbf{q}\|) \delta[b(\mathbf{p}) - u] . \tag{4}$$

Thus, for each $OFF_{i,j}$, two S-OFHs annotated as $S - OFH_{i,j}^x$ and $S - OFH_{i,j}^y$ are constructed for x and y orientation, respectively.

In our approach, left and right slices are selected for computing the S-OFHs excluding middle slice. Four S-OFHs for one figure are ultimately utilized as the motion descriptor. Fig. 4(c) shows the S-OFHs for corresponding action. We can see that S-OFHs can effectively capture the discriminative features for different actions in spatial space.

4   Action Classification

Various supervised learning algorithms can be employed to train an action pattern recognizer. Support vector machine (SVM) [13] is used in our approach. SVM has been successfully applied to a wide range of pattern recognition and classification problems. Compared with artificial neural networks (ANNs), SVM is faster, more interpretable, and deterministic. Moreover, SVM is a classification approach which has been gaining popularity due to its ability to correctly classify unseen data as opposed to methods as nearest neighbor classification (NNC). The advantages of SVM over other methods consist of: 1) providing better prediction on unseen test data, 2) providing a unique optimal solution for a training problem, and 3) containing fewer parameters compared with other methods.

The concatenation of four S-OFHs for each optical flow field in one figure is fed as feature vector into support vector machine. The radial basis function

(RBF) $K(x, y) = \exp(-\lambda \|x - y\|)$ is utilized to map training vectors into a high dimensional feature space for classification.

5   Experiments

This section shows our experimental results on recognizing two basic actions, which are left-swing and right-swing, performed by the player near the camera in far-view scene within broadcast tennis video. By our observations, these two actions occupy about 90% behavior occurred in tennis games.

The test data used in experiments are derived from the video recorded from live broadcast television for one of the matches of Pacific Life Open 2004 in Indian Wells between Agassi and Hrbaty. The video is compressed in MPEG-2 standard with the frame resolution of 352×288. 5 sequences are extracted from the whole video which the total number of frames is 6035 including 1099 for left-swing, 1071 for right-swing. Others are non-swing frames which consist of close-up scenes of players, views of spectators and so on. 56 left-swing actions and 49 right-swing actions are involved in the test sequences.

Two experiments are implemented: one is for action recognition on swing frames; the other is for recognition on swing action clips. To qualitatively gauge the performance, the values of Recall (R) and Precision (P) are calculated. The Accuracy (A) metric is employed to evaluate the holistic performance. Additional 750 swing frames are utilized to train the two-action SVM model.

5.1   Recognition on Frames

First we perform the experiment for classifying 2170 swing frames into two action categories by pre-defined action model. Table 1 summarizes the experimental results which are promising. The Accuracy of the holist is 87.10%. The reason of incorrect recognition is that the player is deformable object of which the limbs make free movement during the action displaying. This will disturb the regular optical flow distribution to make the S-OFHs misreport the motion characteristics in the figure.

Table 1. Experimental results of recognition on frames

	# frame	Recall(%)	Precision(%)	Accuracy(%)
Left-swing	1099	84.08	89.80	
Right-swing	1071	90.20	84.66	
Total	2170			87.10

5.2   Recognition on Action Clips

Based on frame recognition and voting strategy, 56 left-swing and 49 right-swing actions are classified into two categories so as to recognize each action type displayed in the video. This experiment is performed within the framework of

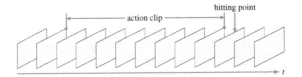

Fig. 5. Location of action clip in the video

multimodal analysis by integrating our action recognition approach with audio-assisted technique in sports video.

First, we employ the audio modalities based method in [14] to detect the hitting ball so as to locate the action clip in the video. As shown in Fig. 5, the frame corresponding to the occurrence of hitting ball is called hitting point. Then the group of frames in the adjacent window before hitting point is selected as action clip. The window length is empirically set to 25 frames in the experiment.

Given f_i which is the ith frame in video clip V, the corresponding human-centric figure obtained by our approach is hc_i. The vote that f_i contributes to V is defined as:

$$Vote(f_i) = \begin{cases} 1 & \text{if } Reg(hc_i) = left - swing \\ -1 & \text{if } Reg(hc_i) = right - swing \end{cases}. \tag{5}$$

where function $Reg(\bullet)$ refers to our action recognition approach. The final recognized action category is determined as

$$Category(V) = \begin{cases} left - swing & \text{if } \sum_{f_i \in V} Vote(f_i) \geq 0 \\ right - swing & \text{if } \sum_{f_i \in V} Vote(f_i) < 0 \end{cases}. \tag{6}$$

Because here are two categories, the equation is just assigned for left-swing so as to avoid the occurrence of marginal classification.

Table 2. Experimental results of recognition on action clips

	# clip	Recall(%)	Precision(%)	Accuracy(%)
Left-swing	56	87.50	90.74	
Right-swing	49	89.80	86.27	
Total	105			88.57

Table 2 shows the experimental results which the Accuracy for all the action clips is 88.57%. Compared with the results on frames in Table 1, it is more satisfactory because the classification is aggregated over the temporal domain by voting strategy. Fig. 6 illustrates some representative frames from the video for the actions recognized by our approach accurately.

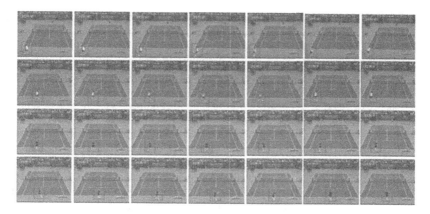

Fig. 6. Experimental results of action recognition for left-swing and right-swing

6   Conclusion and Future Work

An action recognition approach is presented in this paper for motion analysis of tennis player in broadcast video. A novel motion descriptor, which is a group of histograms abbreviated as S-OFHs, is proposed based on smoothing and aggregated optical flow measurements. The noisy optical flow is treated as a spatial pattern of noisy measurements instead of precise pixel displacements. S-OFHs are derived as spatial pattern representation. To recognize the action being performed by a human figure in one frame, support vector machine is employed to train the classifier where the concatenation of S-OFHs is formed as the input feature. The experiments demonstrate that our method is outperformed and the results are promising.

More effective slice partition and elaborate S-OFHs description will be considered in future work so as to include more semantic tennis actions in the recognition framework. Player trajectory is another useful information for semantic analysis and understanding of the game. The integration of action recognition and trajectory tracking will be paid more attention for the research of sport video analysis and enrichment such as event detection, tactic analysis, and 3-D scene reconstruction.

Acknowledgements

This work is supported by Beijing Natural Science Foundation: 4063041.

References

1. Rao, C., Shah, M.: View-invariance in action recognition. In: IEEE Computer Society Conference on Computer Vision and Pattern Recognition. Volume 2. (2001) 316–322
2. Yacoob, Y., Black, M.J.: Parameterized modeling and recognition of activities. In: IEEE International Conference on Computer Vision. (1998) 120–127

3. Miyamori, H., Iisaku, S.: Video annotation for content-based retrieval using human behavior analysis and domain knowledge. In: IEEE International Conference on Automatic Face and Gesture Recognition. (2000) 320–325
4. Cutler, R., Davis, L.S.: Robust real-time periodic motion detection, analysis, and applications. IEEE Transaction on Pattern Analysis and Machine Intelligence **22**(8) (2000) 781–796
5. Efros, A.A., Berg, A.C., Mori, G., Malik, J.: Recognizing action at a distance. In: IEEE International Conference on Computer Vision. (2003) 726–733
6. Zhu, G., Liang, D., Liu, Y., Huang, Q., Gao, W.: Improving particle filter with support vector regression for efficient visual tracking. In: IEEE International Conference on Image Processing. Volume 2. (2005) 422–425
7. Sudhir, G., Lee, J.C.M., Jain, A.K.: Automatic classification of tennis video for high-level content-based retrieval. In: IEEE International Workshop on Content-Based Access of Image and Video Databases. (1998) 81–90
8. Pingali, G.S., Jean, Y., Carlbom, I.: Real time tracking for enhanced tennis broadcasts. In: IEEE Computer Society Conference on Computer Vision and Pattern Recognition. (1998) 260–265
9. Jiang, S., Ye, Q., Gao, W., Huang, T.: A new method to segment playfield and its applications in match analysis in sports video. In: ACM Multimedia. (2004) 292–295
10. Ye, Q., Gao, W., Zeng, W.: Color image segmentation using density-based clustering. In: IEEE International Conference on Acoustics, Speech, and Signal Processing. Volume 3. (2003) 345–348
11. Horn, B.K.P., Schunck, B.G.: Determining optical flow. Artificial Intelligence **17**(1-3) (1981) 185–203
12. Comaniciu, D., Ramesh, V., Meer, P.: Kernel-based object tracking. IEEE Transaction on Pattern Analysis and Machine Intelligence **25**(5) (2003) 564–577
13. Vapnik, V.: The Nature of Statistical Learning Theory. Springer-Verlag, New York (1995)
14. Xu, M., Duan, L.Y., Xu, C.S., Tian, Q.: A fusion scheme of visual and auditory modalities for event detection in sports video. In: IEEE International Conference on Acoustics, Seech, and Signal Processing. Volume 3. (2003) 189–192

FaceMouse: A Human-Computer Interface
for Tetraplegic People

Emanuele Perini, Simone Soria, Andrea Prati, and Rita Cucchiara

Dipartimento di Ingegneria dell'Informazione,
University of Modena and Reggio Emilia,
Italy Via Vignolese 905, Modena Italy
{perini.emanuele, soria.simone, prati.andrea,
cucchiara.rita}@unimore.it

Abstract. This paper proposes a new human-machine interface particularly conceived for people with severe disabilities (specifically tetraplegic people), that allows them to interact with the computer for their everyday life by means of mouse pointer. In this system, called FaceMouse, instead of classical "pointer paradigm" that requires the user to look at the point where to move, we propose to use a paradigm called "derivative paradigm", where the user does not indicate the precise position, but the direction along which the mouse pointer must be moved. The proposed system is composed of a common, low-cost webcam, and by a set of computer vision techniques developed to identify the parts of the user's face (the only body part that a tetraplegic person can move) and exploit them for moving the pointer. Specifically, the implemented algorithm is based on template matching to track the nose of the user and on cross-correlation to calculate the best match. Finally, several real applications of the system are described and experimental results carried out by disabled people are reported.

1 Introduction

One of the human dreams is to live in an intelligent house, full of advanced devices and capable to understand the needs and satisfy them quickly. Nowadays, the technology is mature enough to realize at least part of this dream. Indeed, it is now possible to install in our house sensors of various type that carry out many functions: for example, it is possible to switch a light on when a person enters in the room or open and close windows coherently with the environmental conditions using brightness sensors.

Even though these tools seem unnecessary and expensive for most of the people, for people with motorial difficulties and handicaps they become an indispensable aid for their everyday life. Thanks to these technological aids, these people can do most of the normal things in their house, interacting with it by means of either remote controls or computers, directly from their bed or their wheel chair. For example, they can open and close doors and windows, switch the appliances on and off, write a letter, use a PC, and so on.

T.S. Huang et al. (Eds.): HCI/ECCV 2006, LNCS 3979, pp. 99–108, 2006.

Unfortunately, depending on the gravity of their disability, disabled people can be very limited in movements and cannot easily interact with computers or other devices. For this reason, new human-computer interfaces must be provided.

This paper presents a system called FaceMouse particularly conceived for tetraplegic people. These people, in fact, can only use the head (and with difficulty) to interact with the environment and require special adaptation. FaceMouse uses a standard webcam and computer vision techniques to track the nose of the person and use this to move the mouse pointer (in accordance with the direction of movement of the nose). The mouse pointer is used to select items on special screens, from virtual grids for interacting with the house, to virtual keyboard to allow word processing. The system has been tested on several tetraplegic people and resulted to be very effective and it is currently under commercialization.

2 Related Works

The interfaces between humans and computer proposed in scientific literature and commercial products can be grouped in three different classes: *2D synoptic interfaces*, where the user can activate remote devices selecting the relative icon, *3D virtual world* systems that simulate navigation and interaction with the real world, and, finally, the *classic graphical interface* based on windows.

The systems for disabled people want to reproduce movements of the computer mouse with different methods in order to interface with a computer. They are, typically, based on the tracking of some parts of the human body, indeed used to indicate where to point or where to move. Several approaches have been proposed for making the interface as much natural as possible: they are based on eye-tracking [1, 2], head-tracking [3, 4, 5] or gaze-control [6]. Unfortunately most of these systems are not enough reliable and robust to be usable by a seriously disabled user to pilot the mouse with precision. Moreover, in order to move, for example, the mouse pointer, these systems use a paradigm called *"pointer paradigm"* based on the idea that *"what I look is what I want"*: the user must directly indicate the point of interest on the screen [7, 8]. This task requires a precise control of the used part of the body (e.g, the head), but, unfortunately, many people with disabilities do not have this ability. For this reason, this work proposes the study of a new technique for moving the mouse pointer, exploiting on a paradigm that we called *"derivative paradigm"* based on the idea that *"where I look is where I want to go"*.

Many proposals have been reported in the literature to estimate the motion of visual objects; after a preliminary phase of interesting object searching, most of these techniques employ a tracking algorithm to improve and facilitate the search at the next frame. The used tracking algorithm discriminates among these proposals: there have been proposals for probabilistic algorithms [9, 10], for algorithms based on the Kalman filter [11, 12] and on template matching [7, 8], and many others.

The proposed system, called FaceMouse, exploits a common low-cost webcam to capture images; computer vision techniques are then used to identify different parts of the user's face and to exploit them for moving the mouse pointer or generating a button click. As stated in [13], the best tracking method for user with severe disabilities is based on normalized correlation coefficient since movements in disabled people do not follow any predictable motion model. For this reason, a tracking method based on template matching, where the distance between the portion of the current image and the template is calculated using a cross-correlation function has been developed. Several improvements have been included in order to increase the stability and the robustness of the system.

3 User-Friendly HCI

As above mentioned, for people with sever disabilities, to point at a precise position and maintain it for a while can be very hard. Moreover, the range of movements of the limbs and the head can be limited, preventing the user to point at borders of the image/target. This can be a serious problem, for instance, in Windows-like interfaces, where important elements (such as icons or status bars) are located at image borders. This is even worst for tetraplegic people where the head is used to interact with the environment.

For this reason, the most suitable approach, in these cases, is to use the derivative paradigm described before, in which the movement of the user's head does not indicate the precise position of the mouse pointer, but the direction along which the mouse must be moved. In this way, the user can interact even if he has not a precise control of his head, because he can only do small movements or he suffers from muscular spasms. To detect the chosen direction, we need to track a "good" feature on the person's head/face. Which is the best feature to follow will be discussed in the next section. This section, instead, will describe the user-friendly human-computer interface (HCI) developed for the system.

Initially, the feature is extracted by means of a semi-automatic method. The user is asked to keep the face as much still as possible and an operator (able to use standard mouse devices) selects a point on the current image centered on the chosen face feature (for example, the center of the nose). A squared template centered on this point is used as a model and saved for further matching. Automatic detection of facial features has been explored. For example, the method proposed in [14] (based on stored templates to find the nose starting from the eyes' position) seems promising and have been tried. However, automatic feature initialization comes at the cost of reduced robustness and, due to the particular final users of our system, it is not easily applicable.

The initial center of the feature is used to create a grid as basic interface. More in details, the screen is virtually divided into a grid of 3x3 windows, as reported in Fig. 1.a. The size of each window can be adapted to the abilities of the user: smaller windows are used for users with difficulty to move the head, whereas larger windows are used for users with muscular spasms that have difficulties in keeping the head still in a given position.

After this initialization step, the face feature is tracked to detect movements and understand commands. If the center of the feature is detected inside the central region (indicated with "SW Click" in Fig. 1, where "SW" stays for "stationary window"), it corresponds to the request of not moving the mouse pointer, and if the user maintains the feature in that area for more than a defined time T_{click}, a button click is generated.

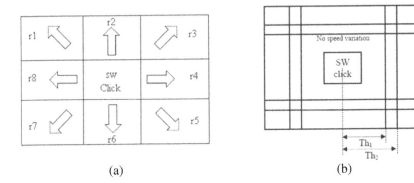

Fig. 1. Example of the grid used as basic interface (a) and for velocity management (b)

If the user moves in a different window (r1,…,r8), the mouse pointer is moved in the corresponding direction. Three different types of mouse pointer's dynamics have been implemented:

- a dynamics with constant velocity, independently from the displacement from the center of the grid;
- a dynamics with constant acceleration, independently from the displacement from the center of the grid; a maximum allowed velocity can be set;
- a dynamics in which the velocity is function of the displacement from the grid's center.

Although the system implements all these three dynamics, the most suitable is the third one. To implement it, we further divided the image grid as shown in Fig. 1.b. Basically, defined $D = \left(d_x, d_y \right)$ the distance of the feature's center from the center of the grid and $V = \left(v_x, v_y \right)$ the velocity of movement to be set for the mouse pointer, $V = \left(0, 0 \right)$ if the user points at the "SW click" zone, and $V = \left(v_x^{base}, v_y^{base} \right)$ (i.e., constant velocity) if the user points inside the first area surrounding the stationary window. For the following zones, the x and y components of the velocity are updated as follows :

$$v_x = \begin{cases} f_1\left(v_x^{base}, a_1, v_1^{max} \right) & \text{if } Th_1 \leq d_x \leq Th_2 \\ f_2\left(v_1^{max}, a_2, v_2^{max} \right) & \text{if } Th_2 \leq d_x \leq w \end{cases} \tag{1}$$

where w is the image width, and f_1 and f_2 are two functions consisting in constant acceleration starting from the first parameter, incrementing at each step of the acceleration given by the second parameter, and upper-bounded by the third parameter. In other words, in the outermost area, the velocity is incremented from v_1^{max} to v_2^{max} with a step of a_2. A similar approach is used for y component.

Summarizing, when the user wants to click on a point of the screen, he must position the mouse pointer on the desired point, return back in the stationary window SW and remain in this area for the time T_{click}. Also the user can disable the click.

Unfortunately, this approach does not work properly for users that can not correctly move the head in all the directions: for instance, people in which the head must be kept fixed by a support or a headrest, and that therefore are unable to even do small movements upwards, or users that can not move the head towards right or left without also moving it down. For this reason, an alternative solution has been implemented: during the setup phase the user (with the help of an operator) chooses a set of points that represent the positions that the user can assume in correspondence of the four directions (up, down, right, left) and of the central position. In this case the selected direction of movement is computed not looking at the position of the feature's center, but at its distance from the pre-defined positions: the positions at minimum distance identifies the selected direction.

This further possibility allows us to increase the usability of the system and the range of potential users.

4 Nose Tracking

As described in the previous section, during the initialization phase, the operator will select for the disabled user a "good" feature on his face. In principle, this feature can be whichever part of user's face (nose, eye, lips, chin, etc.), but, in order to assure a tracking more robust, it should be univocally detectable, and invariant to rotations, translations, and scale changes. It has been demonstrated [8, 15] that the features that better exhibit these characteristics are those represented by convex shapes and the only convex shape easily visible on human face is the nose tip. Assuming light conditions constant between two consecutive frames, normalized cross correlation [16, 17] can be exploited to perform at time t the template matching with respect to the template T^{t-1} at time $t-1$. The template T^0 is that saved at the initialization phase.

Several improvements have been introduced to increase the reliability and robustness of the system. First, the normalized cross-correlation is thresholded to retain only "sufficiently good" matches. The position of the best match (whose score is greater than the threshold) is used to take the next template T^t.

However, this tracking algorithm is very simple and, consequently, it is prone to false matches (mainly due to the face badly illuminated or to over-exposed faces). To reduce false matches, the previous template T^{t-1} is re-aligned to the initial template T^0 as soon as it becomes too different with respect to T^0 (this check is performed once every second).

5 Applications

The proposed system opens to a remarkable number of applications. In the field of aid for disabled people, the possibility to move the mouse pointer allows the following types of application:

1) the use of synoptic interfaces for controlling the house;
2) applications for the interpersonal communication and writing;
3) general Microsoft Windows applications.

For interacting with the house, the system can be interfaced either with an existing system for home automation or directly with the actuators. Fig. **2** shows two examples of the interfaces used in FaceMouse for opening/closing doors and windows, or for switching on and off the different appliances. The user moves on the window corresponding to the chosen device and stays still for a while to generate a button click and open a new interface with specific commands for that device.

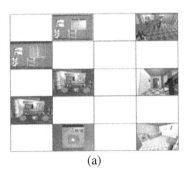

	Doors		Phone
Windows		Lights	
	Radio		Conditioner
Oven		TV	
	Washer		Allarm

(a)   (b)

Fig. 2. Two examples of interface for controlling the house

For example, four automated windows can be controlled by the interface reported in Fig. **3**: they can be simply opened or closed by pushing the corresponding button, or manually opened to some extent by moving the sliding bars.

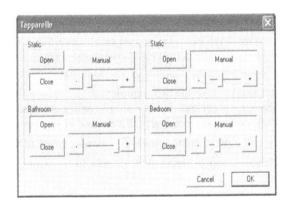

Fig. 3. Interface to control four automated windows

Regarding the interpersonal communication and writing, these are obviously very important tasks for people that sometimes do not have any other way to communicate. Compared with other systems (like supports of transparent plexiglass used as pointers to look), FaceMouse does not need an operator to help the user and it uses a more user-friendly interface, based on the virtual keyboard reported in Fig. **4**. The user can select (by moving the mouse pointer) the single characters to compose words and phrases that the system repeats by using a vocal synthesizer and transmits to the word processor.

A		B		F		G	
	E		J		I		
D		C		L		H	
	O	<	A	•	Y		
M		N		R		S	
	K		Z		U		
Q		P	W	V			T

Fig. 4. Virtual keyboard used in FaceMouse

As above described, the selection of each character is obtained by moving on it and then returning to the stationary window to generate the button click. This procedure can result both too long lasting and not easy for some disabled users. In particular, muscular spasm prevent some categories of users to remain still in the stationary window. To solve this problem and to speed up the process of selecting the characters, several tests with tetraplegic people have been carried out. At the end, two improvements have been included in the system.

The first improvement consists in not requiring to the user to return in the stationary window, allowing to select the character by simply remaining for a while on the corresponding window. This is achieved by means of a voting procedure in which a score is assigned to every character cell and accumulated for every Δt time (fixed by the user) of permanence on the cell. When the accumulated score for a cell exceeds a given value, the corresponding character is selected and the score of all the active cells is reset. The score assigned to a cell during the permanence of the mouse pointer on it is computed by giving higher value when the pointer is close to the center of the cell. This brings to two main advantages: first, it reduces the time necessary to select a character if the user is able to point close to the center, and, second, it reduces the incorrect selections by weighting less "marginal" (and possibly erroneous) selections.

A second improvement is that of suggesting the next most probable character, given the one currently selected. Collecting statistics among different texts, we compute the probability $p\big(c(t+1)\,|\,c(t)\big)$ of having the character $c(t+1)$ selected given that the current character is $c(t)$. Thus, at the center of the virtual keyboard, the five most probable characters are reported (Fig. **5**) and, after every selection, the pointer is automatically moved to the central one that contains the most probable next character.

In this way, if the desired character is one of the five reported, the selection can be obtained quickly with small movements of the mouse pointer.

Finally, our system can efficiently interface with Microsoft Windows operating system allowing the user to run most of the common computer software, and, for instance, to surf on the Internet.

A		B		F		G
	E		<		I	
D		C	•	L		H
•	A	E	I	O	U	•
M		N	Y	R		S
	O		Z		U	
Q	W	P	K	V	J	T

Fig. 5. The virtual keyboard of FaceMouse with, at the center, the five most probable next characters

6 Experiments

FaceMouse has been deeply tested with ten disabled users, in particular with tetraplegic users. After some hour of write training (8-10 hours distributed in some days) with our system, we have asked to the users, habituated to use a scansion system[1], to write the phrase "I am writing with my nose", of 25 characters, with their traditional system and with FaceMouse.

The tests have been carried out with two different dynamics of movement of the mouse pointer: the first one uses a constant acceleration, whereas the second varies the velocity in dependence on the position of the mouse pointer (see dynamics 2 and 3 in section 3).

Analyzing the results reported in Table **1**, several considerations can be made:

1) using the proposed system, the users can write more than two times (without prediction) or more than three times (with prediction) faster than using a traditional system;

2) the best performance can be achieved by exploiting prediction and the velocity dependent on the pointer's position; this is due to the fact that the user can accelerate and decelerate the mouse pointer; however, there can be users for which the constant acceleration is the only possibility;

3) with the prediction system the user can speed up the writing process (by 59% and 25% for dynamics 1 and 2, respectively) with respect to the case

---

[1] In the scansion system the computer proposes one by one all the characters (both on the screen and by means of audio) to the user. When the chosen character is proposed, the user can push a button or similar to confirm the selection.

without the prediction. Moreover, the prediction system almost nullifies the difference in performance between the two dynamics, since the required movements are greatly reduced.

Table 1. Experimental results

Type of movement	Without prediction		With prediction		
	Total time	char/min	Total time	char/min	
Scansion systems	6' 06''	4.1	---	---	**Speed up**
FaceMouse with constant acceleration	3' 03''	8.2	1' 55''	13.1	**59%**
FaceMouse with velocity function of position	2' 19''	10.8	1' 51''	13.5	**25%**

Regarding the computational requirements, FaceMouse does not demand much power and works properly also with PC with a standard 1 GHz processor, processing about 30 frames/sec using only the 50 percent of the CPU time.

7 Conclusions

In this paper we have presented a human-machine interface for helping tetraplegic people (or, more in general, disabled people) to interact with the environment and with other people. The system is based on computer vision techniques, therefore it is not necessary to apply sensors to the body of the users and the interface is user-friendly and adapted to the needs of tetraplegic people.

The tests, performed with several tetraplegic people have demonstrated that the developed system allows the users to write more than three times faster than with traditional systems.

References

1. Beach, G., Cohen, C.J., Braun, J., Moody, G. "Eye tracker system for use with head mounted displays". In: Proceedings of IEEE Intl Conf on Systems, Man, and Cybernetics, vol. 5, (1998) 4348–4352
2. Zhu, Z., Ji, Q., Fujimura, K., Lee, K. "Combining Kalman filtering and mean shift for real time eye tracking under active IR illumination". In: Proceedings of Intl Conf on Pattern Recognition, vol. 4, (2002) 318–321
3. Jilin Tu, Huang, T., Hai Tao. "Face as mouse through visual face tracking". In: Proceedings of 2nd Canadian Conf on Computer and Robot Vision, (2005) 339–346
4. Qian, R.J., Sezan, M.I., Matthews, K.E. "A Robust Real-Time Face Tracking Algorithm". In: Proceedings of IEEE Intl Conf on Image Processing, vol. 1, (1998), 131–135.
5. Toyama, K.. "Look, ma -- no hands! Hands free cursor control with real-time 3D face tracking". In: Proceedings of Workshop on Perceptual User Interfaces, (1998) 49–54

6. Hutchinson, T.E., White, K.P., Martin, W.N., Reichert, K.C., Frey, L.A. "Human-computer interaction using eye-gaze input". IEEE Transactions on Systems, Man, and Cybernetics, 19 (1989) 1527–1534
7. Betke, M., Gips, J., Fleming, P. "The Camera Mouse: Visual Tracking of Body Features to Provide Computer Access for People With Severe Disabilities". IEEE Transactions on Neural Systems and Rehabilitation Engineering, 10(1) (2002) 1–10
8. Gorodnichy, D.O., Malik, S., Roth, G. "Use Your Nose as a Mouse – a New Technology for Hands-free Games and Interfaces". Computational Video Group, IIT, National Research Council, Ottawa, Canada K1A 0R6
9. Verma, R., Schmid, C., Mikolajczyk, K. "Face detection and tracking in a video by Propagatine Detection Probabilities". IEEE Transactions on Pattern Analysis and Machine Intelligence, 25(10), (2003), 1215-1228
10. Moghaddam, B., Pentland, A. "Probabilistic Visual Learning for Object Recognition". IEEE Transactions on Pattern Analysis and Machine Intelligence, 19(7), (1997), 696-710
11. Kalman, R.E. "A new approach to linear filtring and prediction problems". Journal of Basic Engineering, Trans. of ASME, (1960)
12. Oliver, N., Pentland, A.P., Berard, F. "LAFTER: lips and face real time tracker". In: Proceedings of Computer Vision and Pattern Recognition, (1997), 123-129
13. Fagiani, C., Betke, M., Gips, J. "Evaluation of Tracking Methods for Human-Computer Interaction". In: Proceedings of Workshop on Applications of Computer Vision, (2002)
14. Campedelli, P., Casiraghi, E., Lanzerotti, R. "Detection of Facial Features". Technical Report DSI, University of Milan
15. Gorodnichy, D. "On importance of nose for face tracking". In: Proceedings of Intl Conf on Automatic Face and Gesture Recognition, (2002)
16. Horn, B.K.P. Robot Vision, Cambridge MA: MIT Press, 1986
17. Betke, M., Haritaoglu, E., Davis, L.S. "Real-time multiple vehicle detection and tracking from a moving vehicle", Machine Vision and Applications, 12(2), (2000), 69-83

Object Retrieval by Query with Sensibility Based on the KANSEI-Vocabulary Scale

Sunkyoung Baek, Myunggwon Hwang, Miyoung Cho,
Chang Choi, and Pankoo Kim[*]

Dept. of Computer Science, Chosun University,
Gwangju 501-759, Korea
{zamilla100, irune, pkkim}@chosun.ac.kr

Abstract. Recently the demand for image retrieval and recognizable extraction corresponding to KANSEI (sensibility) has been increasing, and the studies focused on establishing those KANSEI-based systems have been progressing more than ever. In addition, the attempt to understand, measure and evaluate, and apply KANSEI to situational design or products will be required more and more in the future. Particularly, study of KANSEI-based image retrieval tools have especially been in the spotlight. So many investigators give a trial of using KANSEI for image retrieval. However, the research in this area is still under its primary stage because it is difficult to process higher-level contents as emotion or KANSEI of human. To solve this problem, we suggest the KANSEI-Vocabulary Scale by associating human sensibilities with shapes among visual information. And we construct the object retrieval system for evaluation of KANSEI-Vocabulary Scale by shape. In our evaluation results, we are able to retrieve object images with the most appropriate shape in term of the query's KANSEI. Furthermore, the method achieves an average rate of 71% user's satisfaction.

1 Introduction

In the oncoming generation of computing, the demand for tools of information retrieval for human sensibilities or tastes and of KANSEI recognition and extraction has been increasing rapidly.

KANSEI in Japanese means by sensibility that is to sense, recall, desire and think of the beauty in objects [1]. KANSEI is expressed usually with emotional words for example, beautiful, romantic, fantastic, comfortable etc [2]. The concept of KANSEI is strongly tied to the concept of personality and sensibility. KANSEI is an ability that allows humans to solve problems and process information in a faster and personal way. KANSEI of human is high-level information, the research of KANSEI information is a field aimed at processing and understanding how the human's intelligence processes subjective information or ambiguous sensibility and how the information can be executed by a computer [3].

---

[*] Corresponding author.

T.S. Huang et al. (Eds.): HCI/ECCV 2006, LNCS 3979, pp. 109–119, 2006.

Study of KANSEI-based image retrieval tools have especially been in the spotlight. However, those researches are still based on the retrieval of lower-level visual information such as features of color, shape and texture [4]. Retrieval of such lower-level information has difficulty catching higher-level information such as intentions or sensibilities of users. And then, in experimentation with human sensibilities, the area of KANSEI-based image retrieval systems has been limited and content-based using visual features such as texture, shape, pattern, and especially color, which are the most popular sources for experiment, or feature-based such as those using recognition system, but such retrievals have had some trouble in checking and recognizing images appropriate for the user's purposes or tastes in higher meaning [5]. To solve this problem, we try the study of KANSEI about shape among visual information.

In order to cope with these limiting barriers, we have attempted to associate visual information with human beings' sensibilities through a relational sample scale, which is made by linking the visual information (color, shape, texture, and pattern) with the KANSEI-vocabulary of human beings'.

First, for the scale we collected and classified the most common shapes and defined what the most standard shapes are. On the other hand, we found a relationship between shape and KANSEI-vocabulary. As a result we were able to produce a KANSEI-Vocabulary Scale for shapes and the related KANSEI-vocabulary. And then we construct the object retrieval system for evaluation based on KANSEI-Vocabulary Scale by shape. In our evaluation results, we are able to retrieve object images with the most appropriate shape in term of the query's KANSEI. Furthermore, the method achieves an average rate of 71% user's satisfaction.

We believe that such a result will allow us to realize a KANSEI-based information system and will be helpful for ontological construction based on visual information and KANSEI-vocabulary. The final purpose of our study is the creation of a KANSEI-Vocabulary Scale based on visual information such as color, shape, texture, and pattern, to form a new KANSEI information system that can understand, retrieve, and recognize human beings' sensibilities and for an ontological system based on visual information and KANSEI-vocabulary. This study develops a vocabulary scale with shapes and sensibilities as one of a series of studies for the purpose, and the scale will be part of the basis of intelligent image retrieval techniques depending on the user's intention and KANSEI.

2   Theoretical Bases for Our Research

2.1   Definition of Shape

Shape means a plane two-dimensional space made by lines and indicates either a 'silhouette' or 'outline'. It is formed by both external angles and a frame axis and expressed the feelings by looking at its inner-shape. Shape has the dimensions of length and width by definition but not of depth. Form is the shape of a thing, its look and bearing, or a body and obtained figure, and is a unity, unified wholeness, or organization which creates a partial order for the entire body of a thing. Form is a three-dimensional trace of the wheels in a dynamic definition. A form is a final shape made by points and lines; a shape is an original feature of a form, and an appearance is a thing made by elaborated combination of the surfaces of the form and its angles. In other words, form means the volume, the three-dimensional mass, or the outline of a thing that can be caught visually. It is also proposed in philosophy that it is the outward pattern of a given thing in a substantial nature.

Geometry is defined as 'the science of dealing with the size and shape of a thing' or 'an area of mathematics limited to mathematical features of space'.

In Rudolf Archaism, a geometrical form is a natural metaphoric or refined form created by ideological thoughts of human beings [6]. This form can be changed into a circle, triangle, square, etc., each of which can be computed mathematically with a ruler and a compass. It can also be called an artificial abstract form changed simply from a complex nature. In other words, this geometrical form gives us systematic, simple and plain feelings, but it originates from nature. Therefore it is occasionally considered to be a concept against natural form.

The precise geometrical forms were made with a method which has a mathematical or physical structure. The method became a standard of measuring beauty, which is now used in related research and help make sense of space intuitively. Although these forms seem to be a bit complex, they can be recognized and reproduced in the same way as the original form. It might not be able to objectively explain the whole contents of the original forms, but it can comprehend their implications in the forms, because the simplicity and rationality of geometrical form are strict rules in themselves. In general, design consists of conceptual elements, visual elements, relational elements, and constructional elements [7].

Table 1. Elements of Form

Elements of form	Constituent elements
Conceptual Elements	Point, Line, Plane, Volume
Visual Elements	**Shape**, Size, Color, Texture
Relational Elements	Position, Direction, Spatiality, Gravity
Constructional Elements	Vertex, Edge, Face

In visual information there are three forms, conceptual, geometrical, and natural form. Geometrical form means an artificial abstract form changed through from into simplicity. The geometrical and natural forms are included organic forms, while natural forms have no defined standard. Therefore all the forms can be classified on the axis of the geometrical form. A shape is created with planes, that is, a shape and a form are created with planes. To show the formation of shape and form, the planes of shape are put into the main elements in the first experiments of our study.

Table 2. Classification of Form

		Soft	Hard	Combination
plane	Cool	Circle	Triangle Equilateral Triangle Isosceles Triangle Isosceles Right Triangle Obtuse Triangle Quadrangle Square Rectangle Rhombus Parallelogram Trapezoid	Segment of a Circle Half Circle Sector Rounded Triangle Rounded Rectangle
	Warm	Ellipse	Polygon	Rounded Polygon
Cubic	Cool	Sphere Hemisphere	Cube Triangular Pyramid Square Pyramid Pentagonal Pyramid Triangular Prism Cuboid Pentagonal Prism Triangular Dipyramid Square Dipyramid Pentagonal Dipyramid	Cone Elliptic Cone Cylinder Elliptic Cylinder
	Warm	Torus	Prism Pyramid Dipyramid Polyhedron	Concurrence Form Opposition Form Piercing Form

2.2 Technique for Application in Object Retrieval

Gradient Vector Flow (GVF) Snake for Detection of Shape's Contour: We use the gradient vector flow (GVF) snake for detection of objects in our proposed system [8][9]. This method begins with the calculation of a field of forces, called the GVF forces, over the image domain. The GVF forces are used to drive the snake, modeled as a physical object having a resistance to both stretching and bending, towards the boundaries of the object. The GVF forces are calculated by applying generalized diffusion equations to both components of the gradient of an image edge map.

The GVF external forces make its snake inherently different from previous snakes. Because the GVF forces are derived from a diffusion operation, they tend to extend very far away from the object. This extends the "capture range" so that snakes can find objects that are quite far away from the snake's initial position. The same diffusion creates forces which can pull active contours into concave regions.

Tangent Space Representation (TSR) for Similarity Measure of Shape: The polygonal representation is not a convenient form for calculating the similarity between two shapes, an alternative representation such as TSR, is needed. For all coming steps it will not use the polygonal representation of the shape, but it will transform it into tangent space [10][11]. A digital curve C is represented in the tangent space by the graph of a step function, where the x-axis represents the arc-length coordinates of points in C and the y-axis represents the direction of the line segments in the decomposition of C. That calls each horizontal line segment in the graph of the step function a step. It traverse a digital curve in the counter clockwise direction and assigns to each maximal line segment in the curve decomposition a step in the tangent space. The y-value of a step is the directional angle of the line segment and the x-extend of the step is equal to the length of the line segment normalized with respect to the length of the curve.

What we got in the former step are turned into their Tangent Space Representation because this technique is invariant, to scaling (we normalize the length of the curve), rotation and translation, and finally the shapes are ready to be indexed [12]. Then, we measure similarity between shapes using indexing values.

3   The Creation of KANSEI-Vocabulary Scale by Shape

3.1   KANSEI-Vocabulary Scale Measurement According to Shape

Now experimental subject shapes are extracted on the basis of the forms analyzed in the previous section. They include twenty shapes. KANSEI words are based on the forms which are collected. We used SD (Semantic Differential) technique through replication or statistics [13]. The process for the creation of a KANSEI-Vocabulary Scale has two steps.

Firstly, after the sample subject group composed of 280 people was shown images of shape, we asked them to describe their feelings with adjectives by looking at each given image. Secondly, all the adjectives collected from step 1 we are classified according to their frequency of use. Thirdly, among the collected words, those that do not express feelings or are not demonstrative words are removed despite their high frequency, with eight words left according to their frequency.

Table 3. The Part of 1st KANSEI-Vocabulary by Shape

Shape Image	KANSEI-Vocabulary
	plentiful, full, mild, perfect, relaxed, safe, satisfied, warm
	offensive, cold, crooked, dizzy, irritative, retrogressive, strange, uncomfortable
	ambiguous, confused, nervous, strange, unique, unstable, vague, worried
	abundant, balanced, comfortable, flexible, liberal, soft, tender, soft and yielding

※ The images shown in the above table can be different from the images used in the real experiment for vocabulary selection.

In the second step, another sample group of 250 people were employed to measure the degree of KANSEI that is show in vocabulary. The standard was five inter valscales. The effects of size, color, aftereffect, and outward environments were controlled to reliably measure the KANSEI scales of each image of shape or line. We are asked to check their own KANSEI scale on the answer sheet after looking at each of the 20 images. Figure 1 shows a sample of measurement of the KANSEI scale: the KANSEI scale of 'plentiful' is 75%, the fourth in five degree section which consists of a 0~100 scale, while '100' means there is no difference between the KANSEI degree and the given KANSEI word, and '0' means there is no similarity between them.

Plentiful

Fig. 1. Example of the KANSEI-Vocabulary Scale

The KANSEI-Vocabulary Scale by shape is produced with the KANSEI scale data measured over the 250 subjects by factor analysis. The purpose of factor analysis is to account variables with the common underlying dimensions which consist of the elements of variables by analyzing the correlations of the multiple variables. In this study the method is employed because it minimizes the information loss of many words, limits to minor factors, and gives a result in essential factors of KANSEI-vocabulary by analyzing the relations among all the KANSEI-vocabulary words and the relations between each shape and its related KANSEI-vocabulary.

3.2 KANSEI-Vocabulary Scale by Shape

The above procedures for the KANSEI-Vocabulary Scale by shape are represented. The procedures produced the result of the KANSEI-Vocabulary Scale by shape as shown in Figure 2.

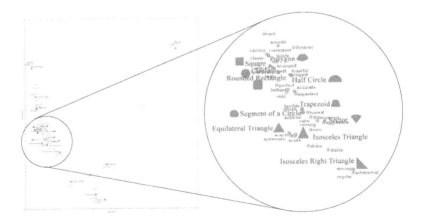

Fig. 2. KANSEI-Vocabulary Scale by Shape

Figure 2 is the KANSEI-Vocabulary Scale of shape (= plane). The result from the procedures of the KANSEI-Vocabulary Scale by shape shows that the features of each shape are closely related to human beings' sensibilities and decides the distance of dimension among the words of the KANSEI-vocabulary. Figure 2 shows that the people of the sample group are more sensitive to curved shapes than the other shapes and felt similar sensibilities to the given shapes. As the values of shape and KANSEI of the given shapes are similar in spite of the different shapes, they are in close proximity. In other words, the factors of curve rather than those of line influence people's sensibilities as well as the factors of shape.

Table 4 represents the KANSEI words and some coordinates of shape on our Scale, which are applied to various areas by means of the distances between the shapes and each KANSEI word and the measure of the distance among the shapes.

Table 4. Scores in Planar Dimension

Name of Plane	Score in Dimension 1	2	KANSEI-Vocabulary	Score in Dimension 1	2	KANSEI-Vocabulary	Score in Dimension 1	2
Circle	-0.537	0.103	plentiful	-0.547	0.107	irritative	3.361	2.325
Ellipse	-0.585	0.720	full	-0.556	0.145	retrogressive	3.361	2.325
Triangle	3.305	2.234	mild	-0.451	-0.028	strange	2.352	0.716
Equilateral Triangle	-0.435	-0.291	perfect	-0.513	0.019	uncomfortable	3.361	2.325
Isosceles Right Triangle	-0.031	-0.527	relaxed	-0.547	0.107	exact	-0.443	-0.303
Isosceles Triangle	-0.397	-0.301	safe	-0.505	0.208	sharp	-0.316	-0.374
Obtuse Triangle	0.332	-1.326	satisfied	-0.547	0.107	threatening	-0.423	-0.308
Quadrangle	1.320	-0.858	warm	-0.547	0.107	precise	-0.443	-0.303
square	-0.532	0.128	cozy	-0.595	0.750	pricking	-0.443	-0.303
Rectangle	-0.663	0.697	crushing	-0.595	0.750	systematic	-0.443	-0.303
Rhombus	1.037	-1.768	dynamic	-0.406	0.262	missing	-0.259	-0.213
Parallelogram	0.967	-1.657	flexible	-0.728	1.291	regular	-0.031	-0.549
Trapezoid	-0.355	-0.135	natural	-0.595	0.750	honest	-0.319	-0.159
Polygon	-0.565	0.211	smooth	-0.505	0.272	stable	-0.190	-0.402
Segment of a Circle	-0.349	-0.157	wonderful	-0.595	0.750	striving	-0.031	-0.549
Half Circle	-0.424	0.082	recursive	-0.595	0.750	substantial	-0.031	-0.549
Sector	-0.213	-0.216	offensive	3.361	2.325	unstable	0.787	-1.123
Rounded Triangle	-0.742	1.012	cold	3.361	2.325	active	-0.404	-0.313
Rounded Rectangle	-0.503	0.098	corrked-curved	3.361	2.325	acute	-0.404	-0.313
Rounded Polygon	-0.846	1.761	dizzy	3.361	2.325	destructive	-0.404	-0.313

4 Architecture and Experiment of the Object Retrieval System

In this section, we propose the architecture of object retrieval and we perform experiment using constructed retrieval system. Our system's purposes are the application of retrieval based on KANSEI-Vocabulary Scale by shape and the evaluation of scale according to user's feedback. Also, this system has made a significant attempt of subjective and semantic retrieval by user's KANSEI. Next figure 3 is architecture of our system.

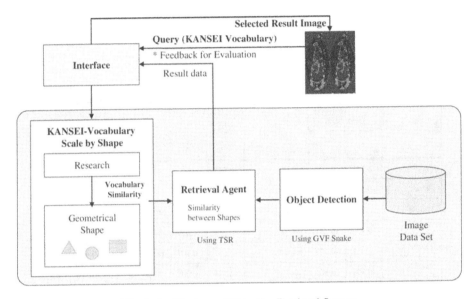

Fig. 3. Architecture of Objective Retrieval System

Architecture of object retrieval show that 1) user queries sensible adjective in the system. And then, 2) find the most nearest geometrical shape about user's query in KANSEI-Vocabulary Scale by shape. Next phase is 3) the measure similarity between finding geometrical shape and object's images in dataset. In 3) phase, we used the method of contour detection and similarity between shapes. Contour detection of object uses the Gradient Vector Flow (GVF) Snake and similarity measure uses the Tangent Space Representation (TSR). Above methods are presented in section 2.2. Using these phases, our system matches most adaptive shape and retrieve the object images based on user's query. Finally phase is 4) user's feedback according to query results in the last step. And we evaluate our scale using the user's satisfaction rate.

We experiment the object retrieval according to 15 queries (KANSEI-Vocabulary) and then measure satisfaction to 20 people-oriented. Our experiment is the meaning of possibility that is applied to retrieval based on KANSEI-Vocabulary Scale and evaluation of our scale by shape.

5   Experimental Results and Evaluation

Using the system of section 4, we evaluate user's satisfaction rate of our proposed KANSEI-Vocabulary Scale. We present the part of experimental results in the following figure 4. User queries KANSEI-vocabulary that is 'comfortable'. User wants retrieval of object that is feeling comfortable. Figure 4 shows the result of running this query.

We orderly retrieve images by the minimum value because of the lower value, the more similarity. The explanation by details is as follows:

$$Min[\alpha \times S_{TSR}(F,I)] = Min[D_{|F-V|} \times S_{TSR}(F,I)] \qquad (1)$$

Where, S is similarity using TSR between F (geometrical shape image) and I (object image). As α is the weight value about each shape, we measure D (distance) between F and V (Vocabulary) in KANSEI-Vocabulary Scale.

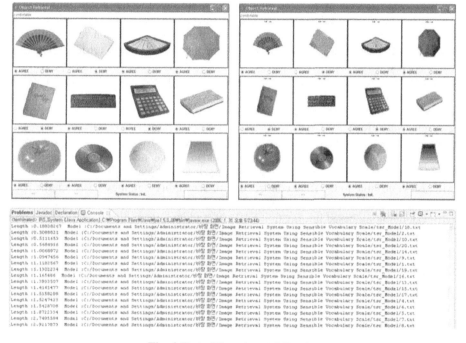

Fig. 4. Part of Experimental Results

The third part of Figure 4, the console tab shows the result of similarity measure using Tangent Space Representation (TSR). We know the nearest shape which is 'rounded triangle' from 'comfortable' and show values of similarity between object images and 'geometrical shape'.

The first two parts of the above figure are result windows. Left window is result of original image and right one is the result image of contour detection. We present 2 results which included images of contour detection. Because it helps user to understand which scale only bases on shape and then its results are considered KANSEI by shape. Image is formed visual information as color, shape, texture, pattern, etc. so, user's satisfaction rate is influenced by other factors.

In this experiment, user's satisfaction indicates much difference from low-rate to high-rate according to KANSEI-vocabulary. The reason of difference is that KANSEI strongly depends on personal disposition and object image includes color, pattern and special design of its, etc.

In experimental result, user's satisfaction is not so high, because it includes other features of visual information. However, we are able to retrieve object images with the most appropriate shape in term of the query's KANSEI. Our scale achieves an average rate of 71% user's satisfaction.

6 Conclusions

In this study we suggested a KANSEI-Vocabulary Scale by observing the relationships among KANSEI words and shapes which are those of the visual information. This scale can be used effectively in KANSEI-based image retrieval according to the user's intentions and in part on the basis of intelligent information research corresponding with KANSEI. We experiment for application of image retrieval based on our scale and construction of object retrieval system for evaluation of user's sensible satisfaction by shape. This experiment helps construct our KANSEI-based image retrieval system, which is applied to various sections including product design and object production, whose main property is shape, to measure user's recognition degree and evaluation.

In our future works, we will expand the range of visual information (not only shape) and will study the KANSEI of combined visual information for intelligent image retrieval. This study continues to work in texture and pattern as well, which will also contribute to the final construction of sensibility-ontology based on the relation of visual information and KANSEI-vocabulary. The results will allow knowledge retrieval, ontology-based information retrieval, and intelligent image retrieval because the KANSEI-vocabulary relation obtained from visual information induces a fixed quantity of KANSEI data.

Acknowledgement

This study was supported (in part) by research funds from Chosun University, 2003.

References

[1] Hideki Yamazaki, Kunio Kondo, "A Method of Changing a Color Scheme with KANSEI Scales," Journal for Geometry and Graphics, vol. 3, no. 1, pp.77-84, 1999
[2] Shunji Murai, Kunihiko Ono and Naoyuki Tanaka, "KANSEI-based Color Design for CityMap," ARSRIN 2001, vol. 1, no. 3, 2001

[3] Sunkyoung Baek, Miyoung Cho, Pankoo Kim, "Matching Colors with KANSEI Vocabulary Using Similarity Measure Based on WordNet," ICCSA 2005, LNCS 3480, pp. 37-45, 2005

[4] Mitsuteru KOKUBUN, "System for Visualizing Individual Kansei Information," Industrial Electronics Society, IECON 2000, 1592-1597 vol.3, 2000

[5] Hyunjang Kong, Wonpil Kim, Kunseok Oh, Pankoo Kim, "Building the Domain Ontology for Content Based Image Retrieval System," Korea information processing Society, The proceeding of fall conference, vol. 9, no. 2, 2002

[6] Rudolf archaism, "Art and visual perception," Mijin Publishing Co., 1995

[7] Wucius Wong, "Principles of Two-Dimentional Design," Van Nostrand Reinhold, pp.5-8, 1972

[8] C. Xu and J. L. Prince, "Gradient Vector Flow: A new External Force for Snakes," In CVPR, pp.66-71, Puerto Rico, USA, 1997

[9] C. Xu and J. L. Prince, "Snakes, Shapes, and Gradient Vector Flow," IEEE Transactions on Image Processing, 7(3), pp. 359-369, 1998

[10] http://www.math.uni-hamburg.de/projekte/shape

[11] Longin Jan Latecki and Rolf LakaÈmper, "Shape Similarity Measure Based on Correspondence of Visual Parts," IEEE Transactions on Pattern Analysis and Machine Intelligence, vol. 22, no. 10, 2000

[12] Alberto Chavez-Aragon, Oleg Starostenko, "Image Retrieval by Ontological Description of Shapes (IRONS), Early Results," Proceedings of the First Canadian Conference on Computer and Robot Vision, pp. 341-346, 2004

[13] C.E. Osgood, G. J. Suci and P.H. Tannenbaum, "The Measurement of Meaning," Univ. of Illinois Press, 1957

Author Index

Lecture Notes in Computer Science

For information about Vols. 1–3878

please contact your bookseller or Springer